Translation Practices Explained

Translation Practices Explained is a series of coursebooks designed to help self-learners and teachers of translation.

Each volume focuses on a specific type of translation, in most cases corresponding to actual courses available in translator-training institutions. Special volumes are devoted to professional areas where labour-market demands are growing: court interpreting, community interpreting, European-Union texts, multimedia translation, text revision, electronic tools, and software and website localization.

The authors are practising translators or translator trainers in the fields concerned. Although specialists, they explain their professional insights in a manner accessible to the wider learning public.

Designed to complement the *Translation Theories Explained* series, these books start from the recognition that professional translation practices require something more than elaborate abstraction or fixed methodologies. The coursebooks are located close to work on authentic texts, simulating but not replacing the teacher's hands-on role in class. Self-learners and teachers are encouraged to proceed inductively, solving problems as they arise from examples and case studies. The series thus offers a body of practical information that can orient and complement the learning process.

Each volume includes activities and exercises designed to help self-learners consolidate their knowledge and to encourage teachers to think creatively about their classes. Updated reading lists and website addresses will also help individual learners gain further insight into the realities of professional practice.

Anthony Pym
Series Editor

Conference Interpreting Explained

Roderick Jones

Routledge
Taylor & Francis Group

LONDON AND NEW YORK

First published in 1998
Second edition 2002
by St. Jerome Publishing

Published 2015 by Routledge
2 Park Square, Milton Park, Abingdon, Oxon OX14 4RN
711 Third Avenue, New York, NY, 10017, USA

Routledge is an imprint of the Taylor & Francis Group, an informa business

British Library Cataloguing in Publication Data
A catalogue record of this book is available from the British Library

Library of Congress Cataloging-in-Publication Data
Jones, Roderick.
    Conference interpreting explained / Roderick Jones.-- 2nd ed.
        p. cm. -- (Translation practices explained, ISSN 1470-966X)
Includes bibliographical references.
  ISBN 1-900650-57-6 (pbk. : alk. paper)
1. Translating and interpreting. 2. Congresses and
conventions--Translating services. I. Title. II. Series.
  P306.2 .J66 2002
  418'.02--dc21
                        2002004946

ISBN-13: 978-1-900-65057-1 (pbk)

Cover design by
Steve Fieldhouse, Oldham, UK

Typeset by Delta Typesetters, Cairo, Egypt
Email: hilali1945@yahoo.co.uk

Printed in the United Kingdom
by Henry Ling Limited

Contents

Foreword   1

1.   Introduction   3
   What is an Interpreter?   3
   What is Conference Interpreting?   4
   The Context of the Conference Interpreter's Work   6
   Definitions and Examples used in this Book   8

2.   Basic Principles of Consecutive Interpreting   11
   Understanding   11
   Analysis   14
        Analysis of Speech Type   14
        Identification of Main Ideas   21
        Analysis of Links   28
        Memory   29
   Re-expression   33

3.   Note-taking in Consecutive Interpreting   39
   Practical Points for Note-taking   40
   What to Note   41
   How to Note   44
   Abbreviations and Symbols   49
   The Language in which to Note   60
   When to Note   61
   How to Read Back Notes   64

4.   Simultaneous Interpreting   66
   The Acoustic Difficulties of Simultaneous Interpreting   67
   The Technique of Simultaneous Interpreting   72
        When to Start Speaking?   72
        Reformulation   80
        The Salami Technique   91
        Efficiency in Reformulation   95
        Simplification   98
        Generalization   101
        Omission (under Duress) and Fast Speakers   102
        Summarizing and Recapitulation   104
        Explanation   104
        Anticipation   105

What if I Make a Clear Mistake?   107

What if the Speaker Makes a Mistake?   108

Avoiding Committing Yourself   110

Metaphors and Sayings   112

Using 'Pat phrases'   114

Intonation, Stress and Pauses   115

Numbers   117

Retour   120

Relay   122

Concluding Remarks on Simultaneous Technique   124

5.   The Pleasure of Interpreting   129

Glossary   131

Bibliographical References   135

Index   139

Foreword

When I was invited to write this book, the idea put to me was that it would fill a gap in the existing literature on interpreting. It was to be a very basic and practical introduction to the fundamental techniques of conference interpreting. As a practising interpreter with an interest in understanding what I do when I am interpreting, and as someone who has been involved for about a decade in interpreter training, I was only too happy to accept the invitation. At the same time, I write only as an interpreter, not as an academic, a theorist or a researcher in the field of translation studies.

The aims of this book are therefore both modest and ambitious. They are modest in that the book can in no way rival with modern theoretical works on interpreting, which draw upon such diverse disciplines as neurolinguistics, computer sciences, semiotics and the philosophy of language. Nor is this book primarily to be read as a teaching manual: it does not tell the reader *how* to acquire the techniques of conference interpreting; it merely sets out to describe them. But that is also why it can be seen as ambitious. When one is interpreting, an awful lot is going on at one time. You are listening, understanding, writing things down, reading documents used in the meeting, analyzing ideas, talking. And all of this while perpetually switching from one language to another, using at least two languages, maybe more. Everything seems to flash by so quickly that it is very difficult to step back and analyze one's work, to know exactly what one is doing and why.

This book is thus an attempt by a practitioner to unravel the processes of conference interpreting and present them in a structured, digestible manner. I hope it will be of interest to four groups of people. First, to students of interpreting and perhaps novice interpreters, who may use the book as a handy compendium of techniques. Second, to teachers of interpreting, who may find in it a codification of a number of the skills they wish to help their students acquire. Third, to colleagues who have asked themselves the same questions as me, even if on a number of occasions I may seem to be stating the obvious. And lastly, to those non-interpreters who have always been mystified as to how an interpreter functions.

For the last nineteen years I have been a staff interpreter for one of the institutions of the European Union. The basic techniques of interpreting, however, are the same whether one is a staff interpreter of an international organization or a freelance interpreter working on the private market, and whichever geographical area one lives and works in. This book is thus designed to be generally valid for all conference interpreting. Of course, the ideas expressed in it are my own and cannot be taken as representing those of the European Union, any of its institutions, or any service of those institutions.

At the end of chapters two, three and four the reader will find some suggestions for practical training activities. These suggestions are put forward in all
modesty. The vast majority of exercises in interpreter training are quite simply
consecutive or simultaneous interpreting. Their usefulness and efficacy as exercises will depend largely on the ability of the trainer to select the right kind of
speech, to achieve progression in the difficulty and typology of speeches, to
target skills to be developed, and to provide useful and above all constructive
criticism for students. Suggestions such as those included in this book can therefore not claim to be a complete guide for trainers.

Crucial moments in interpreter training are often those where a new phase
begins: starting consecutive, or note-taking, or simultaneous. That is why I have
chosen to make suggestions for such moments, calling them 'Getting started...'.
I hope that trainers and students will draw some benefit from them.

1. Introduction

What Is an Interpreter?

Imagine two people sitting in a room. They may be politicians, businessmen or women, trades unionists or scientists. They wish to discuss their work but speak different languages, and neither speaks the other's language well enough for the discussion to be useful. So they call in someone else, who speaks both languages, to explain what each is saying in turn. That person is an interpreter.

This scenario gives a better idea of what interpreting is all about than a pat definition such as 'immediate oral translation'. Interpreting is about communication. The example given above is simplified to caricature but represents the essence of interpreters' work, whether they find themselves in a room with two individuals and two languages or in a large conference hall with hundreds of participants and a multiplicity of languages: people who wish to communicate with one another, and who are prevented from doing so by a barrier.

Clearly, that barrier is first and foremost linguistic. Hence a definition such as 'immediate oral translation'. Interpreters only exist because of that language barrier, and they must obviously have sufficient linguistic knowledge if they are to translate correctly.

But the barriers to communication, and therefore the role of the interpreter, are more than that. People from different countries may not only speak different languages but have behind them different bodies of knowledge, different educations, different cultures, and therefore different intellectual approaches. The fact that such differences have to be coped with independent of the language barrier can easily be seen by looking at a hypothetical discussion between an Englishman and an American. If the Englishman litters his comments with cricketing metaphors the American will have difficulty following, and the American in turn will find it easy to wreak revenge by falling back on baseball and American football.

Communication difficulties are thus much more than pure translation difficulties. The cultural difficulties referred to above can manifest themselves both explicitly and implicitly. Explicitly, a speaker may make references to political, economic, social, academic institutions and systems, intellectual concepts or television catchphrases (the list is endless) that have no direct equivalent in the language of the person they are addressing, and indeed may be totally unknown – and therefore meaningless – to that person. The interpreter's task is to instil meaning into the text for the target audience, if necessary (and if possible) by providing the requisite explanations or even changing the original speaker's references, provided this conveys to the audience precisely what the speaker wanted to say.

Implicitly, and much more insidiously, the intellectual approach to any given question – and therefore the means used by a speaker to express their ideas – will depend on the speaker's cultural background. Certain forms of expression – understatement, hyperbole, irony, etc. – may be difficult or even impossible to reproduce in a different language in given circumstances without betraying the intentions of the speaker. For example, let us just take the adjective 'interesting', when applied by one delegation to a proposal made by another delegation in negotiations. In the mouth of a diplomat given to the habit of understatement (typically a British one), it may mean 'At last, the best idea we've heard for six months!' In the mouth of another diplomat in different circumstances and with the right tone of voice it may well be ironic and mean 'Absurd, how could anyone arrive at such a conclusion?' The interpreter must make their audience understand the real meaning, either through judicious choice of synonyms or by rewording a sentence, or at least through the appropriate tone of voice.

Alternatively, it may be possible semantically to respect both the original form of expression and the original meaning by a literal translation, but the result then sounds downright silly or, still worse, rude. The straightforward forms of address and modes of expression of certain Scandinavian delegates could seem barely civil if put, say, into French or Italian; on the other hand, an artificially flowery style borrowed from another language could make a Swedish interpreter sound ridiculous.

In all of these cases, indeed in all of their work, interpreters must bridge the cultural and conceptual gaps separating the participants in a meeting. This is why, in my opening paragraph, I quite deliberately said the interpreter is called in to *explain* what each of the participants wishes to say in turn. The interpreter should have something of a pedagogical streak, their work being one of continuous explanation and explication. Unlike a teacher, the interpreter does not express their own message; but like a teacher, their task is to make sure that the message is genuinely assimilated by the audience.

What is Conference Interpreting?

The above comments on explanation do not mean that an interpreter is entitled to convey the speaker's message in just any way, using all of the circumlocutions and providing all of the explanations they see fit, and as a corollary taking as long as they like.

The conference interpreter must be able to provide an exact and faithful reproduction of the original speech. Deviation from the letter of the original is permissible only if it enhances the audience's understanding of the speaker's meaning. Additional information should be provided only if it is indispensable to bridge the culture gaps referred to above: it should in no way involve the interpreter's adding their own point of view to that of the speaker.

The conference interpreter, in a way, becomes the delegate they are interpreting. They speak in the first person when the delegate does so, not translating
along the lines of 'He says that he thinks this is a useful idea...'. The conference
interpreter must empathize with the delegate, put themselves in someone else's
shoes, espouse their cause. The male interpreter must be able to say, 'Speaking
as a woman who has gone through four pregnancies...' in a perfectly natural
and convincing manner.

The interpreter must be able to do this work in two modes, consecutive interpretation, and simultaneous interpretation. In the first of these, the interpreter
listens to the totality of a speaker's comments, or at least a significant passage,
and then reconstitutes the speech with the help of notes taken while listening;
the interpreter is thus speaking *consecutively* to the original speaker, hence the
name. Some speakers prefer to talk for just a few sentences and then invite
interpretation, in which case the interpreter can perhaps work without notes
and rely solely on their memory to reproduce the whole speech. However, a
conference interpreter should be able to cope with speeches of any length; they
should develop the techniques, including note-taking, to enable them to do so.
In practice, if an interpreter can do a five-minute speech satisfactorily, they
should be able to deal with any length of speech.

Since time is usually of the essence for meeting organizers, the interpreter
working in consecutive must be efficient. They should in no circumstances take
longer over a given speech than the original version, and as a general rule should
aim at taking three-quarters of the time taken by the original.

The second mode of interpreting is simultaneous. Here the interpreter listens to the beginning of the speaker's comments then begins interpreting while
the speech continues, carrying on throughout the speech, to finish almost at
the same time as the original. The interpreter is thus speaking *simultaneously* to
the original, hence again the name. (Some people say the interpreting is not
genuinely simultaneous as the interpreter is by definition fractionally behind
the speaker throughout, arguing then that this mode should be called 'quasi-
simultaneous'; yet this appears to be a rather futile quibble, and we shall continue
to use the term 'simultaneous'.) In most cases nowadays simultaneous is done
with the appropriate equipment: delegates speak into microphones which relay
the sound directly to interpreters seated in sound-proofed booths listening to
the proceedings through earphones; the interpreters in turn speak into a microphone which relays their interpretation via a dedicated channel to headphones
worn by the delegations who wish to listen to the interpreting. However, in
some cases such equipment is not available, and simultaneous interpretation is
whispered (so-called 'chuchotage'): one participant speaks and simultaneously
an interpreter whispers into the ear of the one or maximum two people who
require interpreting services.

Clearly, simultaneous interpreting takes up less time than consecutive.

Moreover, with simultaneous it is much more feasible to provide genuine multilingual interpreting, with as many as six languages (UN) or even eleven
(European Union). Given these advantages and the proliferation and widening
membership of international organizations, more and more interpreting is being
done in simultaneous. But all conference interpreters should be able to work in
both modes, as one can never rule out being called upon to work in consecutive.

From this brief description it is clear that whether working in consecutive or
in simultaneous, the interpreter has first to listen to the speaker, understand and
analyze what is being said, and then resynthesize the speech in the appropriate
form in a different language (the difference being that in simultaneous the interpreter begins resynthesizing before having been able to hear the totality of the
speech to be analyzed – a problem we shall return to). It is this continuous
analysis and resynthesis, a constant active intellectual apprehension of speech
and its meaning, that enables the conference interpreter to walk the tightrope
between travestying a speaker's message by over-literal translation and betraying it by inaccuracy, which may in turn be involuntary or due to excessive liberties
taken with the text by the interpreter.

It is also clear that conference interpreters work in 'real time'. In simultaneous, by definition, they cannot take longer than the original speaker, except for
a few odd seconds. Even in consecutive they are expected to react immediately
after the speaker has finished, and their interpretation must be fast and efficient.
This means that interpreters must have the capacity not only to analyze and
resynthesize ideas, but also to do so very quickly and when working under stress.

The Context of the Conference Interpreter's Work

Besides the technical difficulties of consecutive and simultaneous interpretation – which are the object of much of this book – the interpreter is faced with
the problem of working in different contexts and with a vast range of subjects.

One may work for international organizations, or one may be turned more
towards the private sector, offering one's services on an ad hoc basis to private
companies, trades unions, ministries, political parties and all kinds of scientific
and academic conferences and seminars, as well as the countless meetings organized by the ever-growing cohort of international lobbies.

In an international organization interpreters are nowadays likely to work essentially in simultaneous. In the vast machines that these organizations have
tended to become (one thinks of de Gaulle's 'grand machin') they generally
remain an anonymous voice, with little or no personal contact with the delegates they are working for. If one works regularly for the same organization,
either as a member of staff or as a freelance interpreter who prefers to take
regular employment from it, then a certain amount of the work becomes routine: one is acquainted with the procedures, the topical issues, one may even

work for a given committee or on a given specific topic on a regular basis. But such 'routine' is not the general rule. As more and more questions assume an international dimension, in other words with globalization, the international organizations find they are dealing with an ever wider range of issues, and consequently interpreters must cope with them too.

On the private market there is little risk of work becoming routine. The relationship between the interpreter and delegates or meeting organizers is less that of an employer-employee type and more of a client-service provider one. There is a better chance of personal contact with delegates. If the delegates are satisfied with the work of a particular interpreter they will ask to have them again in future, thus providing a degree of continuity. But many private-market meetings occur only irregularly and a wide range of clients is necessary to ensure sufficient income for any interpreter dependent only on the private market. Further, interpreters in the private market have to be prepared to deal with practically anything under the sun: it is there that one tends to find the most difficult technical conferences, including scientific and medical ones.

Another major difference is between bilingual or multilingual meetings, since this directly affects the demands made of interpreters. In bilingual meetings, whether in consecutive or simultaneous, delegates and meeting organizers often prefer to have interpreters who can work both ways between the two languages. For example, if the meeting is in English and Japanese, organizers would prefer to have individual interpreters who each work from English into Japanese and from Japanese into English. In multilingual meetings, say with six languages, it is clear that individual interpreters cannot be working into a multiplicity of languages. In such cases, interpreters will work only into one language, usually their mother tongue, but translate out of a number of the five other languages used in the meeting. The training, language knowledge, experience and skills required in each of these two circumstances are different, and for some interpreters the choice may have to be made whether to specialize in one kind or the other. Of course, the two types are not mutually exclusive: some colleagues are in the happy position of being able to interpret into two languages and from a fair number of languages.

Some meetings may be extremely general in content, and others highly technical. For general meetings the interpreter may need no specialized vocabulary at all and perhaps no specific knowledge other than what one may easily acquire by reading the daily press. This does not mean, however, that such meetings are necessarily easy. Their very blandness can make them awkwardly elusive to the interpreter, who may have to deal with the finest nuances of meaning, so fine sometimes as to seem to exist only in the mind of the speaker (for example a distinction made between 'where appropriate' and 'where necessary').

Going through every degree of technicity one can then arrive at the other end of the scale, where meetings are impossible without preparatory reading of background documentation, a briefing given by participants to the interpreters before proceedings begin, and the use in the course of the meeting of a specially prepared technical glossary. This highest degree of technicality is thankfully rare, but interpreters just have to learn to live with it. Note that 'technical' here does not just mean 'scientific' in the commonest use of that word. A meeting may be technical because it refers to nuclear technology or the tempering of steel, but it may also be technical because of legal content or because it deals with leading-edge questions relating to the provision of television services.

In conclusion, the one thing the interpreter will not lack in their work is variety. Apart from the differences mentioned above, the interpreter will be confronted by different physical working conditions, from the cosy conversation of two individuals, through the proverbial smoke-filled room of political and diplomatic negotiations, to the large lecture theatre with hundreds of participants, and above and beyond that the field trips where one has to shout above the machines in an industrial plant or trudge through the mud to describe the merits of organic farming *in situ*. Above all, the interpreter will be faced with a literally infinite range of subject matters. The same basic skills will always be required, but the interpreter has a vast field to work in and must therefore have broad general knowledge and be intellectually curious, always seeking to widen that general knowledge.

Definitions and Examples Used in this Book

Before moving on to the techniques of consecutive and simultaneous interpretation, a few words are needed on the definitions and examples that I will be using (in addition to the more detailed terms explained in the Glossary at the end).

Interpreter here will always mean a conference interpreter. *Consecutive* and *simultaneous* will sometimes be used as nouns, meaning consecutive or simultaneous interpretation; such use should be clear from the context. *Speaker* will always mean the original speaker to be interpreted and should not be confused with the interpreter, even if the latter is 'speaking'.

The *source language* means the language in which a speech is made in the original, and out of which it is to be interpreted. The *target language* is the language into which it is to be put, and which the interpreter therefore speaks.

A *passive language* is a language out of which an interpreter is capable of interpreting. An *active language* is one into which they are capable of interpreting. An interpreter's 'working languages' are the sum of their active and passive languages. It should be noted that *source* and *target* on the one hand, and *passive* and *active* on the other, do not have the same meaning, the first two referring to a specific circumstance, the latter to the general interpreting capability of an individual.

The *mother tongue* here means the best active language. An interpreter should have total mastery of their mother tongue, that is, they should have the ability to express themselves fluently, grammatically and precisely, with accurate and extensive vocabulary, such that they can reflect finer shades of meaning on a broad range of topics. For some people, their 'mother tongue' is not technically the language of their mother, or either of their parents, nor even of their country of birth (due perhaps to an education in a different language, or because the family emigrated and the child or adolescent adopted the language of the host country). This is immaterial; we shall simply use 'mother tongue' for the first active language, without further explanations. It should be noted that by the criteria just mentioned some rare, lucky interpreters can claim to have two mother tongues. Others, for the purposes of competent interpreting, have no real mother tongue and can be described as alingual. These, however, are among the people who never make it to being a conference interpreter.

Retour means an interpretation where the interpreter is working into an active language other than their mother tongue. It is possible to have an active language which is not up to mother tongue standard, but to use it actively requires special technique. To simplify life for themselves many interpreters choose to work into a second active language only out of their mother tongue.

Relay refers to a situation where a meeting is multilingual and not all the interpreters understand all of the languages used. Let us say that the languages of a meeting are French, Russian and Spanish. The Spanish interpreter understands French but not Russian. The French interpreter understands all three languages. When a speech is made in Russian, the French interpreter will interpret it into French. The Spanish interpreter then interprets not the original Russian, but the interpretation into French of the colleague, working thus at one remove. Here the French colleague is called the 'relay', as is the interpretation into French itself. Relay can be used in consecutive and in simultaneous.

Lastly a word on the examples we shall be using. All of them are totally fictitious, since this helps avoid involuntary indiscretion about meetings which actually occurred. Some of the examples may seem a little stilted, yet they have the advantage of being tailor-made for the point they are illustrating. Sometimes for examples to work they need to be fitted into a mini-scenario. These will be presented as briefly as possible, so the reader is invited to make a little effort of imagination to understand the situation the interpreter is in.

Examples of texts to be interpreted will be given solely in English. When we discuss the problems arising out of different grammatical and syntactical structures in different languages, the source language text will be presented in 'English', but using the grammar of a different language. The whole will be accompanied with the necessary explanations in English. For example, if we wish to illustrate the famous difficulty of simultaneous interpretation of German sentences with the verb at the end we will not give an example in German, but an example might read: 'This Dutch proposal aiming at a reinforcement of

controls can we, following consultation with our Finance Ministry, support.'
This makes strange reading in English. However, we hope that by sticking to
English the text will remain accessible to colleagues and students whatever their
working languages, and that examples will have as much general validity as
possible, rather than just applying to certain language pairs.

2. The Basic Principles of Consecutive Interpreting

To express ideas clearly and effectively, you must first have them clear in your own mind. It follows that if you wish to re-express someone else's ideas without having the possibility of repeating them word for word – which is the case for the interpreter – then you must make a clear, structured analysis of them. And to make that analysis you have to understand the individual ideas that are the basic building blocks of a speaker's line of reasoning.

In order, then, the three basic stages of a consecutive interpreter's work are *understanding*, *analyzing*, and *re-expressing*. These three notions have to be looked at in turn.

Understanding

The 'understanding' we refer to here is not of words but of ideas, for it is ideas that have to be interpreted. Obviously, you cannot understand ideas if you do not know the words the speaker is using to express them, or if you are not acquainted sufficiently with the grammar and syntax of the speaker's language to follow the ideas.

In connection with the notion of 'not knowing words', it is best to address here what is probably one of the two commonest questions put to conference interpreters by non-interpreters: 'What do you do if you do not know a word or an expression that you hear in a speech?'

The answer to this has already been partially given when we say that the interpreter has to understand ideas, not words. It may well be perfectly possible to understand a speaker's meaning without actually understanding every single word and expression they use, and without having to reproduce all of those terms in the interpretation. For example, imagine a delegate says:

> I don't think that the advisory committee is the appropriate forum for discussion of this point. What is important is that the groundwork be done in the technical working parties, in order to prepare the basis for a decision in the executive committee.

Let's assume the unlikely, namely that the interpreter understands neither *forum* nor *groundwork*. Yet this does not prevent them from understanding that (1) the advisory committee is not the right place to discuss the matter, and (2) the question has to be properly prepared for the executive committee by the technical working parties. The interpretation is possible without all the words and without changing the meaning.

There are other occasions, however, where a word is too important to be skated round in this way. Let us say that Norway is being discussed and the motorway network is referred to:

> Given the topography of the country, the construction of motorways has
> been very expensive. The Norwegians have found the solution to their
> financing problems by imposing tolls. And these tolls are pretty expen-
> sive. The roads are wonderfully built, a pleasure to drive upon, with
> beautiful scenery, but when the poor driver gets to the end of their jour-
> ney and has to pay the toll, they certainly feel that their wallet is much
> lighter.

The key word here is *toll*, and if the interpreter does not know it they can hardly
avoid it. But the interpreter can also benefit from working in consecutive. By
the time they start interpreting they will have heard the whole speech, and should
have been able to deduce the meaning of *toll* from context, given the number of
clues they have. Thus, again, it is possible for the interpreter to work satisfactorily, indeed in this case totally accurately, without their having known in advance
all the vocabulary used by the speaker.

Two further points should be made here. First, interpreters must accept that
there are times when they do not know a word or an expression, can neither
avoid it nor deduce its meaning from context, and are consequently stuck. In
those circumstances, the interpreter, particularly in consecutive where there is a
straightforward human contact with the delegates, must admit their ignorance,
and, if necessary, clarify the question with the delegates. The interpreter cannot
be expected to be a walking multilingual dictionary-cum-encyclopaedia and has
a perfect right not to know certain things. On the other hand, the interpreter
does not have the right to 'betray' the delegates by missing things out or guess-
ing at meanings in order to hide their ignorance.

Second, in order to understand meaning without knowing *all* the lexical items,
and still more in order to deduce meaning from context, the interpreter must in
any case have a thorough knowledge of their passive language(s). Arguing that
interpreting is possible without knowing all the words should not be distorted
into the argument that an interpreter does not need to know their passive languages properly.

To return to the question of 'understanding', we must stress that pure linguistic understanding (what we might call 'comprehension'), although necessary,
is not a sufficient condition for the interpreter to be able to re-express ideas
efficiently in another language. Interpreters must be able to seize meaning in a
split second, and must therefore listen constantly in an active, attentive way,
always asking themselves 'What does the speaker *mean*?'

This active, attentive listening is quite different to other forms of listening,
and has to be learned by the interpreter. Compare first of all active listening
with the passive listening of everyday life, in a conversation or in front of our
radio or television set. Imagine that the following is broadcast on the radio:

> Despite the apparent confidence shown by the government in the latest
> measures it has proposed to boost the economy, business confidence re-
> mains low and the consumer climate is gloomy.

The man in the street who hears this is likely to note there are new government
measures to boost the economy, may well assume they have already been put
into effect (although the journalist tells us these are only proposals) and that
they have not worked (which is logically nonsense). Apart from the errors contained in this 'understanding' of the news item, the casual listener may also
ignore the government's attitude and the *detail* of the description of the de-
pressed economic mood. That is passive listening.

Let us now assume exactly the same text is put to a member of the government by a journalist during an interview broadcast live. The member of the
government will not, one assumes, listen passively, but will listen actively solely
with a view to defending the government's position, and will latch upon anything in the journalist's words which help. A reaction may be :

> As you say, these are only the latest proposals. They are part of a greater
> overall mobilization of all of the government's efforts, indeed of the na-
> tion's efforts...

The politician turns, wilfully and almost literally, a deaf ear to anything in the
journalist's comments which it is in the government's interest to ignore. This is
a form of active listening, but a very selective one, where the listener picks up
only those elements it is useful to pick up with a view to replying. It is a form of
listening that is far from limited to politicians, and need not be adversarial. In
business dealings, in diplomatic negotiations, in collective bargaining between
industry and trades unions, participants may have their antennae out for just one
crucial piece of information, and will recognize and register it when it is given.

The interpreter cannot afford such luxuries. Whatever the speaker says, everything must be attended to and carefully sifted, even if ultimately – indeed
inevitably – the interpreter concludes that certain elements in the discourse are
not important. Let's return to our example, which for convenience will be repeated here:

> Despite the apparent confidence shown by the government in the latest
> measures it has proposed to boost the economy, business confidence re-
> mains low and the consumer climate is gloomy.

In the opening four words there are three notions, all of which may be important, and to which the interpreter has to be attentive: (1) the confidence of the
government ('confidence'); (2) it only *seems* confident ('apparent'); (3) the
implied distancing of the speaker from the government view ('despite'). The

first thing to be said is that all of these notions should appear in the interpretation (our man in the street noticed none of them and the politician ignored them). Second, depending on the context, on the speaker's tone of voice, etc., the interpreter may conclude that a particular idea is crucial, for example idea number two. The interpretation might then begin:

> The government *seems* confident about its latest proposals to boost the economy. However, ...

And so on, every element of the speech being consciously registered and processed by the interpreter.

One should not deduce from an analysis such as this that the interpreter is thinking about each word individually in detail. On the contrary, the interpreter must not pay attention to individual words as words, but must listen to the overall sense of a speech, identifying the ideas that are expressed through the words (which are mere vehicles for meaning, and intrinsically of no interest for an interpreter). Moreover, the interpreter, we must remember, is working in real time. The speaker will speak at a normal pace, making no allowances for the interpreter, who at the end of the speech will be expected to translate instantaneously: there is no time for a detailed, conscious, semiological analysis in the heat of the action.

However, what this example does show is the need for constant active listening. The interpreter must listen to *everything* and keep asking: 'What does the speaker mean? What are the ideas they want to express?'. This form of listening is not a natural gift; it is something that has to be learned and trained. Even when it has been learned it requires great powers of concentration and stamina in any but the shortest of meetings held in consecutive, hence the need for interpreters at all times to be fit and mentally alert.

Analysis

Analysis of Speech Type

Working from this active listening, the interpreter may proceed to an analysis of the speech. The first question to ask oneself is what kind of speech is being dealt with. Speeches may be of many different kinds. If they are presenting a reasoned, logical argument, they can be differentiated into two subsidiary categories: reasoned arguments that present both points of view on a question, weighing up pros and cons before arriving at a synthetic conclusion, and those that are a sequence of logical deductions leading inexorably to the only possible conclusion (from the speaker's point of view). On the other hand, speeches may be narrative, adopting a purely chronological sequence. They may be descriptive, which could mean anything from describing a scene or an event to a detailed statistical presentation, for example of the economic situation of a company or an industrial sector. They may be polemical, where the speaker is hell-bent on convincing the audience, sometimes to the detriment of logic, courtesy or even honesty. And speeches may be purely rhetorical, where the detail of content is secondary, maybe even irrelevant, the main aim being to sound impressive, notably through elegant style and a number of cultural references, and perhaps to pay tribute to somebody or some organization (a dinner speech to thank the host country of a conference, for example). The 'speech' may even be stonewalling, the speaker going to some considerable lengths to hide their point of view or to withhold information, thus speaking – conceivably at great length – without communicating anything, which may pose major difficulties to an interpreter, who has first to recognize such a type of speech and must then remain similarly non-committal.

These examples of speech types are certainly not exhaustive, but are probably the most common interpreters are faced with. It is necessary for the interpreter to make an analysis of the speech type as this will influence both the fine-tuning of their listening and most certainly the style and content of their interpretation. Let's look at these points in turn.

First, if a speaker is putting forward a reasoned line of argument the interpreter must pay particular attention to the logical connections between ideas. If it is the kind of speech weighing up pros and cons, then the interpreter must know what is a pro and what is a con, and spot the turning points between them: all of the uses of *but*, *however*, *on the other hand* and so on, which are so many warning beacons to the interpreter.

In such a speech the speaker has basically two options: either to navigate to and fro between the two points of view being examined, or to present one argument in its entirety then make a major caesura and present the other point of view. In both circumstances the interpreter must follow the movement of the speaker. In the former case you have to take great care to follow the sinuous development of the argument and make it perfectly clear to the audience which point fits in where, otherwise the interpretation will become a rather indeterminate magma of little use to the delegates.

Let's take an example. A sociologist is commenting on the desirability or not of technical progress applied to agriculture:

> Mechanization and the widespread use of insecticides, herbicides and chemical fertilizers have essentially freed Europeans and North Americans from real food shortages, from hunger. But they have also brought with them their problems, notably ecological ones. We can compare ourselves to other continents and feel privileged. But will the price not be too high one day? Are we not overproducing, making neither economic

nor environmental sense? But if others throughout the world still experience famine, surely we should exploit all means available, in order to
share our riches with them...(and so on for another five minutes).

You may feel this is not a particularly good speaker, but the passage is typical
of countless speeches to be interpreted. Practically every sentence expresses a
position contrary to the preceding one, and there are not necessarily the convenient markers (such as *but*) every time to warn us. The third sentence (*We can...*)
is not flagged as contradicting the second one, but from the context it is clear
that it does. On the contrary, *but* seems to be reserved initially for the sentences
expressing the 'anti-technical progress' point of view, although following the
two rhetorical questions it is used to introduce a sentence expressing the 'pro'
point of view. There is absolutely no fixed system governing the expression of
this kind of non-linear thinking: the interpreter has to unravel it all, noting the
relationships between ideas and seizing on the explicit markers which facilitate
that task.

As mentioned, a 'pro and con' speech may be more clearly presented, with
first one side of the story, then the other. In such a speech it is absolutely crucial
that the interpreter identify (and then correctly re-express) the central linchpin
of the speech. If an interpreter spends two minutes defending one point of view
and then spends another two saying the opposite *without warning the audience*
that this is an alternative, then those depending on the interpretation for understanding are going to have considerable difficulties following.

You should not assume that delegates are necessarily kind enough to highlight the fact that they are now changing tack. The interpreter may be lucky and
get *However* or *Notwithstanding my previous comments* served up on a plate.
But words and phrases such as *Clearly, Obviously* and *It is true that* may also
be casually used to introduce a contradictory line of argument. In such circumstances the interpreter must be doubly vigilant. First, they must recognize that
this is the turning point used by the speaker to change direction. Second, when
making their interpretation they must make sure that this is absolutely clear to
the audience. If a speaker argues black, throws in *clearly* and then argues white,
it is perfectly legitimate, indeed desirable, for the interpreter to argue black,
then make a significant pause to let people know this is the end of a section of
the speech, and say something quite unequivocal such as: *However, one may
take the opposite view...* before proceeding to argue white. This does not betray
the speaker's meaning and it makes understanding that much easier for those
who depend on the interpreter. Note that many a consecutive interpretation is
better than its original in this respect.

The second form of logical, reasoned speech type is the one-sided argument,
presenting deductions and syllogisms to prove a point. If this is well expressed
it should by definition be reasonably easy to interpret, as it should provide a

coherent, understandable argument. However, to do justice to the speaker the interpreter must be very vigilant again, paying attention in particular to *all* the logical links of the speech: *as, given that, therefore, consequently, because, thence*, etc. can all be key words. The problem with this kind of speech is that precisely because it is so logically constructed, with A leading to B leading to C and so on, if the interpreter makes an error or misses out one stage in the reasoning, the whole construct comes tumbling down, and the audience, without having understood a word of the original, will know there's a problem with the interpretation. That's why *all* the logical links have to be carefully watched.

In such a speech the speaker may well try to make things clearer by providing an explicit structure, numbering or lettering ideas and sections. This is a godsend to the interpreter and should always be latched upon and exploited to the full. If, as often happens, the speaker is not fully faithful to their own outline – for example announcing that there are three reasons why, and then presenting four – the interpreter should take this in their stride and quite simply announce four reasons, or not announce the number in advance but structure the interpretation around the reasons actually given. The last thing to do is embarrass the speaker by pointing out the discrepancy! The point should be raised with the speaker only if the interpreter is genuinely in doubt as to what has to be said and needs clarification.

Of course, a speaker may provide no such convenient structuring but the interpreter, having fully understood the speech, is nevertheless in a position to provide it. In such a case, the interpreter is more than entitled to make structure explicit in order to make things clearer for the audience. For example, if a speaker reels off three arguments in favour of a given position, without numbering them, the interpreter may begin: *This is for three reasons*, and then number the points as they are presented: *First... Second... Third....*

Our third type of speech is the narrative, chronological speech. A chronological narrative may be history, the story of a country, or an international organization over the last fifty years. But it may also be the chairperson of a meeting summing up the situation at the outcome of the last meeting, the procedure followed since then, including the activities of various sub-committees and the procedure envisaged for the immediate future. Whatever the subject of the narrative, it goes without saying that the interpreter must pay due attention to time phrases, dates and verb tenses. People want to know what happened when. It may make all the difference in the world if the Ball-bearing Lubricant Sub-committee *has* submitted its report or *will* submit its report.

If a speaker does not respect chronology in the original, it is up to the interpreter to decide whether this is deliberate or involuntary on the part of the speaker. If there is a reference back to the League of Nations when the creation of the UN has already been discussed, for purposes of comparison, then the interpreter may choose to follow the speaker. If the accession of Greece to the (then)

European Community is brought in after that of Spain and Portugal in a way that is confusing and can only be ascribed to the speaker's having forgotten to mention Greece at the right moment, then the interpreter is well advised to respect history, slipping in Greece in its rightful place. The speech will be clearer for the audience, and the original speaker, if they understand anything of the interpretation, will be grateful to the interpreter for having quietly corrected the error.

The fourth type of speech is descriptive. This may be deceptively difficult, as a description is ultimately a juxtaposition of a number of items, not necessarily determining one another. For example, the description may be of recent economic trends in a country:

> Exports have risen, and so have imports. The trade deficit is growing, although the current account deficit remains stable thanks to tourism. Rising unemployment and consistently high interest rates are a source of worry for the government, but the Central Bank continues to warn about inflationary pressures.

Practically no element in this extract follows logically from any other element or combination thereof. Exports have risen, but imports could just as well have fallen. With both rising, there could be a trade deficit, balance or surplus, and no way of knowing which way it is moving. The same for the current account. The only 'logical' things (in the sense of logically determined by other elements in the speech) are the attitudes of the government and the Central Bank, and the implied conflict between them about monetary policy (this last element, however, remaining implicit).

The only thing an interpreter can do with descriptions is concentrate as hard as possible, decide what is the most important information, and remember and note down as much as possible of that.

As we mentioned, speeches may be polemical in nature. To be polemical does not necessarily mean being illogical, discourteous or dishonest, but it may involve any one of these three things, or a combination of them, and in any case does imply a vigorous defence of one position, and clear rejection of the opposing point of view. To deal with such a speech the interpreter must be sensitive and flexible while remaining faithful to the speaker. Remember that the interpreter in a way 'is' the speaker. They must espouse the speaker's point of view, conveying not just the content of the original but also the tenor of comments, the intensity of feeling. Therefore, even if the interpreter feels the speaker is sacrificing logic or truth to their cause, it is not for the interpreter to question that: interpreters must have the intellectual flexibility to reproduce something they find highly questionable, and they must do so to the best of their ability, trying to be as convincing as possible.

At the same time, we must not forget that an interpreter is what we might call a 'communication professional'. It is their role to help people come together and understand one another. This is a very moot point, but it can be argued – and we would argue – that there are occasions when an interpreter may tone down comments in order to take the sting out of a meeting: repeating tactless or rude comments may in some cases be in the interest neither of the speaker, nor of the addressee, nor of the proceedings in general. To know when to do so is a very delicate affair, and can certainly not be 'taught' in a book like this. Nevertheless, we may consider two examples, one where editing by the interpreter is unjustifiable, another where it may be defended.

Let's assume that in multilateral international negotiations, one delegation links granting a concession on point A to gaining satisfaction on point B, which would be to the detriment of another delegation, who consider point B to be extraneous and any reference to it unfair. This latter delegation says to the first one: 'We refuse to put up with blackmail of this nature!'. *Blackmail* is a pretty strong term to use; a number of delegations in the room will have understood the accusation; the delegation being accused of blackmail considers its attitude as part of the normal horse-trading of a negotiation, and would, in a monolingual environment, certainly wish to defend itself against the accusation. Assuming the delegation depends on the interpreter to understand the accusation, it would be totally unfair to tone down the text, editing the key word, and thus depriving the accused party of the possibility of defending itself. Just imagine if the interpreter falls into that trap and says something bland such as 'We object to this link being established', then the accused delegation runs the risk of being made to look totally stupid by an urbane response such as: 'We understand your objection, but still feel that some give-and-take is required on this matter'.

On the other hand, let's assume that in a discussion – the context is irrelevant – one party puts forward an idea and another delegation exclaims: 'You have to be pretty stupid to suggest something like that!'. Here the interpreter would be well advised not to translate the text faithfully. The speaker may well be biting their lip at such an impulsive reaction; a literal translation would poison the atmosphere and perhaps jeopardize the entire meeting. The interpreter may choose to say, 'That's not the brightest suggestion we've heard on the subject', which conveys, perhaps with the right dose of irony, the message of total opposition to the proposal without being offensive. The discussion may continue, serenely one hopes, and the speaker could secretly be blessing the interpreter for having saved the situation. Mercifully, such incidents are rare, but most interpreters will at some stage in their career have to exercise such judgement.

Finally, speeches may be rhetorical, the one occasion when form becomes more important than content. Typical occasions are dinner speeches and farewell speeches from departing diplomats or members leaving a committee. In such speeches it is more important to capture the spirit than the exact detail of the content. Whereas in technical fishing discussions it is important to get all four fish right – cod, herring, whiting and saithe – here it is not necessary to repeat faithfully on every occasion 'our common historical, cultural and artistic heritage'. The heritage may sometimes become cultural but not artistic or vice versa, and nobody will bat an eyelid.

This, however, does not mean that the interpreter can relax and that such a speech is plain sailing. First, such speeches usually contain specific references involving proper names and titles. These references may be made to people present or at least personally known to those present. They may involve, for example, thanks to the host for hospitality or congratulations to a departing chairperson for their good management of procedure. In such circumstances it is catastrophic if such references are not picked up and included in the interpretation. Moreover, the interpreter must be on their guard, as the references to the people concerned may be fairly veiled. The speaker might make it easy by referring to 'our host' or 'Mrs Smith'. But the reference could be more obscure, say to the 'Vice-Chancellor', a title not previously used and which it transpires is another hat worn by the Italian ambassador. Or the speaker may become disconcertingly familiar, suddenly talking of 'Brian', 'Marie-Christine' and 'Dieter', and the poor interpreter, who is not on first name terms with the delegates, has little idea of who is being referred to. In all such cases the interpreter must make sure the references are in.

References may also be made to historical figures and events, literature, works of art and so on. These too must all be picked up. If, for example, a French speech to a partly English-speaking audience includes the words *Shakespeare* and *Hamlet*, then the interpretation must also include those words, even if the interpreter is not sure what part of *Hamlet* is being referred to or what its relevance is. The English speakers will certainly have picked up those two words, indeed they may be literally the only two words they have understood, and if they do not hear them in the interpretation they will feel cheated.

Second, rhetorical speeches can be difficult precisely because of their form. Speakers may use images, metaphors and similes, flowery language, tell anecdotes and jokes. The interpreter has to mobilize all their resources in their mother tongue, or other target language, in order to do justice to such speakers, to render not just the sense, but also the tenor of the original.

Of course, some 'rhetorical' speeches may be pure stonewalling. For such speeches the interpreter should follow the speaker as closely as possible. Speaking at length while saying nothing is a considerable art and any deviation from the text by the interpreter may well instil a meaning which the speaker wished to avoid.

This is in fact an illustration of one of the golden rules of interpreting, valid in all circumstances: *the interpreter must make no substantive addition to a speech.* By adding something the interpreter is by definition saying something the speaker did not say, thus making a mistake. The interpreter may be factually right. The point may be intrinsically interesting. But the participants are not interested in what the interpreter thinks or says. At best, adding something just wastes time, if the addition is ignored by everybody. Worse, it may distract participants' attention away from the points actually made by the speaker. Worst of all, an interpreter's comment may be taken up by a participant for discussion, plunging the meeting into confusion.

This point might seem to run counter to the basic idea of an interpreter as a communication bridge between people separated by culture as well as by language, helping people to understand one another by providing the appropriate explanations and information where requisite. This really only shows that interpretation is not an exact science and that there are occasions when interpreters have to show discretion and make judgements.

For example, let's assume a British speaker mentions the House of Commons to a non-British audience. Perhaps everyone present knows what the term means, and no explanation is needed from the interpreter. It may also be, however, that for some non-British people the House of Commons means nothing at all, in which case the interpreter can add, 'the lower chamber of the British parliament'. This is perfectly acceptable as a useful piece of information to help people understand. But let's assume that subsequently the same speaker refers to the House of Lords, and that the interpreter adds: 'the unelected upper chamber of the British parliament'. That's going too far. By adding one word – 'unelected' – the interpreter has introduced a substantive idea that may convey an impression quite unwanted by the speaker. The fact that the interpreter is technically correct is neither here nor there.

As mentioned above, the list of speech types given here is far from exhaustive. Moreover, life is not so simple: most speeches are hybrid and share characteristics from two or more speech types. However, it is useful for the interpreter to identify, be it only instinctively, such speech types, and to use this general analysis in the fine-tuning of the particular analysis necessary for each individual speech, and to which we can now turn our attention.

Identification of Main Ideas

In order to be able to interpret a speaker's ideas you must know first of all what is important in their comments and what is secondary, what is essential and what accessory. The interpreter, in analyzing a speech, must therefore identify the main ideas, and *know* they are the main ideas.

This in a way is self-evident: the speaker's ideas are to be reproduced in the interpretation, and the most important ideas must be included. However, as has already been stressed, the interpreter's role is also to reflect the tenor, the spirit, the underlying significance of a speaker's comments, as well as the literal sense. This can only be done if ideas are given their relative importance in the inter pretation. Many a poor consecutive is sub-standard even though 'everything is there', since everything is given the same weight and no particular elements or threads are highlighted, making it difficult for the listener of the interpretation to know what the speaker is really trying to say.

A second reason for systematically identifying the main ideas is that the interpreter may be under duress because of the intrinsic difficulty of the speech or the speed of the speaker, and will therefore have to omit one or more elements of the original. If the interpreter just misses out things at random the interpretation will be pretty well useless. However, if they have analyzed the speech and include all the important elements, linking them correctly and coherently, missing out only what they know to be details, then the interpretation will not be perfect but can still be adequate for the purposes of the meeting.

Third, the recall of the speech necessary in consecutive will be easier if the interpreter has a number of key ideas around which to structure their recollections, rather than having a sequence of ideas all on an equal footing. Again, we shall return to this under 'memory'.

Fourth, it is useful for all interpreters to be capable of providing a summary of a speech, since when delegates are really pressed for time the chairperson may actually ask explicitly for the interpreter to give not a full interpretation but a summary.

What are, then, the main ideas of a speech? Before answering this question we must bear in mind that 'main ideas' implies a hierarchy of relative importance of ideas. One or more ideas may be central to a proposition. Others in the proposition may be 'secondary', but this does not mean they are unimportant to the point where they do not need to be interpreted. These 'secondary' but nonetheless significant ideas may in turn be more important than a third category of ideas, which in terms of content of a speech may seem quite extraneous, digressions, or mere illustrations. But even these may need to be interpreted either to render the colour of a speech, brighten it up with an anecdote or make a theoretical point easier to understand by a practical example. Thus, when in this section ideas are referred to as 'accessory' or 'secondary', this should not be misunderstood as meaning unimportant to the extent that such ideas need not be interpreted.

To turn to the question of locating the main ideas, it is impossible to lay down a hard-and-fast rule, but generally one can say that delegates need answers to the three basic questions: who? what? when? Or more specifically: who does what, and when, and who says or thinks what.

Let's take an example:

> The Secretary-General has put forward to the member states a new pro-
> posal for the reform of the functioning of the UN. US State Department
> sources confirmed yesterday that, although in principle they recognized
> the need for reform, they did not see it being along the lines suggested by
> the Secretary-General.

This, in its crudest form, could be reduced to:

> The Secretary-General has made a proposal for UN reform. The US
> has said it is against the proposal, although it is in favour of reform in
> principle.

That is a simplification based on a *subject-verb-object analysis:* 'who did what?'
and 'who said what?' The fact that the proposal is a 'new' one is not part of that
analysis, nor that it has gone to the member states, nor that it concerns reform of
the 'functioning' of the UN, and so on.

Note that this kind of subject-verb-object analysis is always in terms of the
meaning, not of individual words or grammatical categories. Let's take another
example:

> The Socialist spokesman on the environment attacked the government
> yesterday for failing to...

For a word-level grammar, the subject of the sentence is a noun, *the spokesman*, with *Socialist* functioning as an epithet relating to it. For the interpreter
the subject is most definitely *the Socialist spokesman*, as the spokesman's
being Socialist (rather than Conservative, Christian Democrat, etc.) is what
defines him.

One of the key questions to be answered in any speech, as we have just
mentioned, is 'who says/thinks what?' In our example this question is dealt
with thanks to the subject-verb-object analysis: 'The US has said...'. However,
points of view are often expressed in a speech in a much more incidental way.
A delegate may say, 'In our view', 'According to the Secretariat', etc. Allusions
to points of view may be still more oblique: a report may be referred to by a
speaker, who then quotes extensively from it, without ever explicitly ascribing
the quotations to the report. In all such cases the interpreter must try to be
aware of whose point of view is being represented, and make it clear to their
audience. There is a world of difference between (1) stating as an objective fact
that 'US import duties on Japanese electronic goods are too high'; (2) being
overtly subjective. as in 'We feel that US import duties...'; and (3) ascribing a
point of view to someone else, as in 'The Japanese government feels that US
import duties...'

Those elements in a speech that fall outside both the subject-verb-object analysis and an analysis of points of view are at best secondary. The first elements that may be seen as secondary are individual epithets and adverbs. Thus in the sentence, 'The traditional, wooden houses and baroque churches left by the early Spanish settlers were all devastated by the earthquake of a magnitude of seven on the Richter scale', the epithets *traditional*, *wooden* and *baroque* are all of secondary importance. The most important thing is that an earthquake has destroyed the buildings.

However, as always, the interpreter must work from context. If the sentence now becomes: 'The traditional, wooden houses were all devastated, but the baroque, stone churches left by the early Spanish settlers somehow remained standing', it is clear that a contrast is being drawn between *wooden* and *stone*, and the relative resistance of these materials to earthquake. This has to be highlighted accordingly. In this case, though, we also see the usefulness of proceeding by first identifying main ideas, to which secondary ones may then be attached. The main thing the interpreter registers mentally is 'houses destroyed, churches not', and then relates to the nouns their characteristics or qualities, in this case wooden and stone respectively. It is notable that other descriptive elements not pertinent to the contrast between the fate of the different types of buildings – 'traditional', 'baroque', 'left by the early Spanish settlers' – although they should of course be included in the interpretation, have a still more subsidiary importance in the interpreter's analysis.

The interpreter must also be wary of 'false epithets', that is, adjectives presented as epithets but which have predicative value. For example, the delegate who says, 'This *excellent* proposal is one which will help my government considerably', is, with the help of intonation, really expressing two propositions: 'This proposal is excellent', and 'It will help my government considerably'. The predicative value of *excellent* should be reflected in the interpretation.

Similar comments may be made on adverbs as on epithets, with a particular comment on adverbs of time. We said above that delegates want to know who does what and when. This means that adverbs of time, although not part of a subject-verb-object analysis, tend to be of rather more importance than other adverbs. Even so, of still greater importance are the tense and mode of the verb itself. A delegate may need to know whether something happened one or two weeks ago, but it is even more fundamental to know whether an event is past, present, future or hypothetical. The interpreter must therefore take care to note not just what the meaning of a verb is, but also its tense and/ or mode as appropriate.

By definition, examples are secondary to the main thread of an argument. When faced with an example, the interpreter has two things to do. First, they must indicate clearly that it is an example. If a delegate says, 'Some European countries, such as France, Spain and Portugal, have expressed concern about what they see as unfair competition from Californian produce and have requested a higher level of protection', the words *such as* can make all the difference. If the interpreter merely says, 'Some European countries – France, Spain and Portugal – have expressed...', this means the three countries cited stand on their own. Assuming that other Mediterranean countries such as Italy and Greece agree with them, the interpreter will have provided a wrong translation.

Second, the interpreter may have to decide whether examples are purely illustrative and can be edited, or whether they have some intrinsic importance and should be dealt with exhaustively. It is possible for speakers to be overlong, giving unnecessarily lengthy illustrations or lists of examples, and for the efficiency of proceedings and clarity of understanding it can be preferable for the interpreter to edit examples of a purely illustrative nature. Let's assume that in a seminar of theatre directors on Shakespeare a participant says, 'The historical plays, beginning with *Richard II,* right through *Henry IV part 1, Henry IV part 2, Henry V, Henry VI part 1, Henry VI part 2, Henry VI part 3, Richard III* and up to and including *Henry VIII,* have to be seen in the political context within which Shakespeare was writing'. Given the topic of the seminar, the composition of the audience and the prior knowledge they may be supposed to have, the speaker is being long-winded and patronizing to the point of rudeness. A consecutive interpreter is entitled to abridge, but should keep in some element of illustration, for example saying, 'The historical plays, beginning with *Richard II* and right through to *Henry VIII,* have to be seen...' Again, the interpreter must show sensitivity to the speaker's message and use existing background knowledge. Let's assume now that the speaker said exactly the same thing but added the word *particularly* before '*Richard III*'. The word *particularly* must clearly function as a kind of warning beacon to the interpreter, who may also be aware that *Richard III* is a very politically motivated play, and who must mention it as a key example.

On the other hand, elements presented as examples may have an intrinsic importance, in which case the interpreter must do their utmost to include everything. Take a trades-union spokesman who says to the representatives of industry, 'We need to look at all aspects of the organization of working time, for example the overall reduction of working hours, greater flexibility, job-sharing and compensation for flexibility, in particular for night and weekend work.' This is less an illustrative list than a catalogue which needs to be expressed in its entirety. Moreover, the importance of examples will sometimes be obvious in context. A list which seems illustrative may be given at the outset of a speech, but then the speaker returns to each of those points systematically. In those circumstances the interpreter can benefit to the full from working in consecutive and will find it easier to judge to what extent examples have to be taken up in full.

The last group of elements in a speech which may be called secondary and which it is important to comment upon is made up of all kinds of asides, parentheses, digressions, comparisons, even verbal redundancies. It is obvious, logically speaking, that such things are secondary, but in the heat of the fray the interpreter sometimes has to keep a cool head to avoid being misled by them. Speakers may wrap up the essence of what they are saying to such an extent, sometimes taking longer over non-essentials than essentials, that the interpreter risks losing sight of the structure and thread of a speech. The best way to illustrate this, and other points we have made about identifying and analysing the main ideas, is to take a longer example of a speech.

A British delegate in a conference with a wide international participation, but in the absence of any Russians, is reflecting on the advisability or not of extending NATO to the east to include countries in the so-called former Soviet bloc:

> Thank you, Chairman. As a number of speakers have said already, this is a very difficult problem, but it is also an important one, so I should like to add some comments if I may. I think we all realize we are faced with a dilemma. Indeed, one can't help feeling like the nobility under Henry VII, in my own country, when faced with the tax demands of that king, and who ended up being placed, so to speak, on Morton's fork. Whatever we do, in a way it will be wrong.
>
> For it is clear that the countries of central and eastern Europe have quite legitimate expectations, which we cannot deny forever, about their position in Europe, about their security, about their integration into the community of western democracies with free market economies. And we are all the less well placed to deny these aspirations as we, to a large extent, have, if not created, at least endorsed and encouraged them. Moreover, we also have to recognize that for these countries integration with western Europe is seen as a whole. They see themselves in the long term, and sometimes in the not-so-long term, as natural members of the European Union, then of the WEU, given its close links to the European Union, and, again because of the ideological community of spirit and purpose of these organizations, of NATO.
>
> On the other hand, to extend NATO to include all of the countries of central and eastern Europe, up to the frontiers of the former Soviet Union, but to exclude Russia, will look like an expression of mistrust, if not aggression, to Russia.
>
> Chairman, this is an urgent matter. It cannot be dealt with by putting off people again and again. We must simply recognize the contradictory interests at stake, and not bury our heads in the sand like an ostrich, and reconcile those interests as best we can. We must offer our neighbours in central and eastern Europe the principle of membership of NATO now, but accept that negotiations for the timetable and modalities of their accession will have to be all-party, that is, will have to include Russia, in order to offer Russia appropriate compensation, and in order to make

clear to Russia that the enlargement does not constitute a threat to its interests.

In this speech the British delegate is presenting, however succinctly, an argument with a thesis, an antithesis, and an attempt at a synthetic conclusion. The main ideas the interpreter must identify and bring out in the interpretation are those three components to the argument. As to the question of point of view, this is an easy speech in that throughout it is clearly all from the speaker's own perspective, not ascribing ideas to anyone else.

The first paragraph is practically all a verbal redundancy. The speaker merely tells us this is an important and seemingly insoluble problem. The reference to fifteenth-century English history has to be seen most definitely as an aside, and it will be up to the interpreter's discretion, depending on the target language and the composition of the audience, to decide whether Morton's fork is a meaningful and useful notion or whether the passage should not be abridged or simplified.

The second paragraph is the argument for enlargement. There are two main points, with one sub-point to the first of these. First point: the countries concerned have a perfect right to integrate with western Europe, it is in their interest; sub-point: we have ourselves encouraged such an attitude. Second point: integration with western Europe has to be seen in a broader context than just NATO. These two main points have to be sorted out by the interpreter and expressed clearly. The interpreter must avoid being distracted by refinements and corrections such as 'we, to a large extent, have, if not created, at least endorsed and encouraged', and 'in the long term, and sometimes in the not-so-long term'. Again, this is not to say that such elements should remain untranslated. Simply, the interpreter must know they are of lesser importance, not focus their attention on the speaker's qualification or attenuation of ideas, and state them straightforwardly in their interpretation.

The third paragraph is the argument against, and is stated so briefly and directly that there is really no processing of information necessary for the interpreter.

As to the conclusion, this may be summed up as: 'the matter is urgent; we must say now there will be enlargement; Russia must be involved in negotiations about enlargement, to reassure it and offer possible compensation'. There is much rhetoric about accepting the truth, but that should be dealt with on its own merits, that is, precisely, as rhetoric.

To sum up, the interpreter must pick up the half-dozen or so ideas that make up the backbone of this speech and lay sufficient emphasis on them in the interpretation; verbal redundancies should be cut down to a minimum; digressions, extraneous comparisons and rhetoric may be kept in the translation but should have the right relative weight in the overall context of the speech; and the interpreter must not let the form of the speech – qualifying clauses, hesitations, corrections, verbal prevarication – distract them from the substance.

Analysis of Links

The first key to understanding a speech is the identification of the main ideas; the second is an analysis of the links between those ideas. A speech is not just a sequence of juxtaposed sentences. The sentences are related to one another in a particular way, and it is this relationship that determines the overall meaning of a speech.

The number of ways in which ideas may be linked is in fact fairly limited. First, there may be a logical consequence: *The import duties imposed on Korean cars are excessive and discriminatory. Therefore, they must be reduced.* Consequence may be expressed very clearly, as in this example, or with words such as *consequently* or *as a result*; it may also be expressed more casually and by sometimes ambiguous words such as *so*.

Second, there may be a logical cause, as in: *The American government has been exerting greater pressure on the Colombian authorities, because the illegal import and consumption of cocaine from that country is again on the increase.* The interpreter must likewise register all words like *as*, *since* or *due to*.

Third, ideas may be sequential, following on from one another, but without logical cause or consequence. In such cases sentences may be simply juxtaposed or the ideas linked with the little word *and*. Here it must be noted that when ideas are simply juxtaposed – where the link is what we might call a 'zero link' – the interpreter must not fall into the trap of creating another link artificially. Although key words such as *because* and *therefore* should not be omitted, to create a link where there is none in the original is an equally serious mistake. Nor should the interpreter abuse the word *and*. A series of sentences strung together by *and...and...and...* is poor style, which may irritate the audience; worse, the resulting formlessness of the interpreter's output may actually make the overall sense of a speech difficult to follow.

The third type of link – sequential – is particularly important to note in comparison to the fourth type, namely links which actually oppose two ideas. In this set of links there are different sub-sets that the interpreter should also be aware of. Such an opposition may be simply offering an alternative or casting a different light on a question: *The strong Mark may not be good for our exports, but is has contributed to holding down inflation.* It may also be a flat contradiction: *you claim that you have been unable to fulfil your export quotas; but our figures show that imports from your country are actually double the quotas.* On the other hand, the opposition need not imply a logical contradiction but may contrast two situations: *Certain countries have attempted to apply strict monetary and fiscal discipline, whereas others have felt it more important to stimulate the economy.* Lastly, an opposition may simply attenuate a previous idea: *This is a very useful proposal. However, I don't think we should get too excited about it....* In all of these cases it is important for the interpreter to reflect the right form of opposition expressed by the speaker.

Apart from these four basic types of links – logical consequence, logical cause, sequential ideas, opposition – ideas may be linked by certain forms of speech that the interpreter should exploit. For example, the speaker may put rhetorical questions. If the speaker asks 'Why?' and then goes on to answer their own question, the interpreter, depending on the target language, may choose to translate the rhetorical question literally, but may also choose to omit it for stylistic reasons and reproduce the idea by beginning *This is because....* Alternatively, a speaker coming to the conclusion of their remarks may signal this by beginning a peroration with *Chairman, ladies and gentlemen....* Again, it is up to the interpreter to exploit this structuring element in the speech, even though it does not have much intrinsic meaning, to make the interpretation more clearly structured and therefore easier to follow for the audience.

Memory

A consecutive interpreter listens to a speech and then reproduces it in a different language. This means the interpreter must be able to recall ideas, in other words they must call upon their memory. It may be objected that if the interpreter takes adequate notes during the speech they should not need to rely upon memory. We shall discuss note-taking later, but suffice it to say for the moment that it is impossible for an interpreter to rely solely on good notes, and that even if it were possible, it would not, in our view, be desirable. The consecutive interpreter must therefore cultivate the use of short-term memory.

In the context of interpreting, 'memory' has to be more closely defined. Normally memory means, of course, 'remembering things', remembering dates in history, names, telephone numbers, vocabulary in foreign languages. This kind of memory can be most useful for passing exams at school and university, and can also be useful in other professional activities. But this kind of learning by rote is not the kind of memory useful for an interpreter. Indeed, 'memory', it could be argued, is a misnomer for the intellectual faculty to be exercised by the interpreter. For the interpreter must order ideas in their brain so as to be able to recall them and reproduce them in a significant way.

How can an interpreter order and stock ideas in their mind so as to facilitate recall as much as possible? Part of the answer lies in the use of mnemonic techniques. Through these the interpreter attaches notions or 'labels' to the ideas they wish to recall. Let's look first at the use of a general mnemonic technique that does not apply to an interpretation. A candidate for a job is asked to recall twenty words given to them orally, without being allowed to note down anything.

The list is :

Father – house – tie – authorize – chemical – anxiety – love – photograph – mouse – plate – Wagner – sunshine – filing-cabinet – erase – spectacle – shark – presidential – Prague – undergo – teeth

The candidate recalls all but three words: *authorize*, *erase* and *spectacle*, but the seventeen words recalled are in a different order from that in which they were given. When asked how they remembered so many, the candidate explains, 'I imagined my father, wearing a tie, coming into the house. He looked anxious, because he thought he could smell chemicals. I remembered I loved him and thought of the photo of him on my desk at home. I imagined him standing in front of a filing-cabinet, and looking at a mouse in a plate. For Wagner I remembered an open-air performance I saw on television from the south of France. I just remembered *shark*, but I think it was because I had an image of it from the film *Jaws*. *Presidential* and *Prague* somehow fitted together for me because I admire Vaclav Havel a lot. *Undergo* and *teeth* also fitted together because I just saw myself sitting in the dentist's chair "undergoing" treatment.'

Here the candidate has put tags in a quite arbitrary way on a sequence of unconnected words, and used the tags to recall the words. Interpreters are not faced with a sequence of unconnected words, but meaningful discourse. They must therefore attach these tags to ideas rather than individual words. One way of doing this is to try to visualize what the speaker is saying. The hypothetical job applicant in our example invented arbitrary visual images as a memory aid; the interpreter will not use arbitrary images, precisely because they are faced with meaningful discourse which in some cases can be visualized. Clearly, the kind of speech that lends itself most to this technique is a description or narration concerning physical, observable events, for example a description of a natural catastrophe:

> Hurricane Henry moved into northern Florida early yesterday morning. Nearly half a million people have had to be evacuated as the 200 km per hour winds uprooted trees, tore roofs off some houses and completely demolished less sturdy ones. In coastal areas many boats were submerged by the 10 meter swell, while others were beached and left stranded with their hulls ripped open.

Such a passage can be better remembered and therefore interpreted if the interpreter sees the scene in their mind's eye than if they take the words as lexical items – *trees*, *roofs*, *houses*, etc. – which need their counterpart in the target language.

However, it is not just such obviously visual texts that can be dealt with in this way. Geographical locations can also be recalled by trying to imagine them on a map. In the example above the interpreter could easily have in mind the East Coast of the United States and pick on it an area to the north of the peninsula of Florida. Such a technique is particularly useful if a whole series of related geographical locations are referred to:

> In the long term the idea is to develop a European high-speed railway network with Paris at its centre. A line to the north will reach Brussels, where it can branch out to the east to Cologne, or continue further north to Amsterdam and later even Hamburg. To the south-east the line through Lyon will enter Italy through Turin and reach through Rome and Naples right down to the toe of Italy. And in the south-west a link up with Spain via Barcelona and then Madrid will make it possible to extend the network down to Seville.

Now, it would theoretically be possible to try to remember all these cities as a list, but it will be so much easier to have in one's mind a map of western Europe and to imagine the cities and the lines traced out between them on that map.

Interpreters may find that even rather more arid texts that at first sight do not contain any particularly strong visual elements can usefully be dealt with via visualization. For example, in discussions on customs tariffs a Czech delegate may say: *The sectors we are particularly concerned about are coal, glass and footwear.* Again, you can take these words as abstract notions, but it may also help some interpreters to see in their mind the pithead of a mine, typical cut Bohemian glass and a pair of shoes.

There are of course limits to the technique of visualization as a mnemonic aid. A speech may be so abstract that no amount of effort will produce a visualization of the notions expressed. In such cases, some interpreters may feel better tagging the ideas with numbers rather than visual images. The interpreter may note, as a speech progresses, that there are three main points; that under the first point there are two examples; that in the second point, refuting the first, there are also two examples, echoing the first two; and that in the conclusion drawn from the opposition of the first two points, three specific consequences are drawn. Some interpreters do not like working in this way, finding the numbering distracts them from the actual substance of ideas. It is also true that if the speaker does not divide their own speech up rigorously it may be difficult to identify points to number so clearly; and if one reproduces such a cut-and-dried structure in the interpretation, where it was absent in the original, one risks distorting the speaker's message.

Yet it can also be an immense help to tick off points in your mind, using numbers to do so. More important, this brings us to the most important part of 'memory' – that is, ordering of ideas with a view to their recall – for a consecutive interpreter. When talking about analysis we stressed the importance of concentrating on two key elements: the main ideas and the links between those ideas. By concentrating on these the interpreter will automatically be thinking of the speech in terms of its structure. And the speech will be easier to recall, even in points of detail, if you have its structure clear in your mind. To make the structure easier to retain, it may be useful to number the basic elements – main ideas or sections – in your mind. The interpreter can then use the basic structure of the speech as a kind of skeleton on which to hang the other elements of the speech. Let's consider an example:

> We feel that the free-market approach to provision of social services, with its insistance on minimum state intervention, freedom of competition, deregulation and cost-effectiveness, though theoretically sensible has proven in practice to be a disaster. And why? Because in all cases, hospitals and other health services, public transport, education, no free competition has been really possible. The service user has been faced in any one given area by a single private service provider facing no effective competition, which is able therefore to function as a monopoly. Those who are too destitute to pay for private services may, if they are lucky, fall back on residual public services, starved of money by the government and therefore unable to provide an adequate service. No real competition, no free market. And we are left with a dual society. Those who can afford to be exploited by private service-providing monopolies, and those who cannot and therefore have to put up with inferior services.

This may be remembered in outline as:

> Free-market approach (4 components) to social services failed in practice.
> Why? No competition (3 areas quoted).
> Single private service provider.
> Therefore monopoly.
> Only 'competition' from underfunded public sector.
> No competition = no market.
> Dual society (describe).

This skeleton can then be used by the interpreter to provide a fuller version as follows. The free-market approach is characterized by the interpreter, using the four components mentioned by the speaker. The idea that it has failed 'in practice' induces in the interpreter's mind the corollary that it is 'sensible in theory'. The areas where lack of competition is cited can be recalled as health, education and transport, 'health' inducing in turn the word *hospitals*. The single service provider can function as a monopoly because of the lack of 'effective competition'. The 'residual' public services cannot compete because underfunded and – logical consequence – unable to provide 'adequate' service. No real competition, no free market. Dual society: the nature of the dual society to be filled in (logical conclusion to the whole argument).

Thus, from a telegrammatic recollection of the basic structure of the speech the interpreter is able to flesh out the information so as to provide a complete version of the original. They do this by mobilizing all possible means at their disposal. They use the basic structure as a starting point from which to induce other ideas of finer detail. They may perhaps number elements to facilitate re-call (the three areas of social services cited, for example). They may use visualization (the residual, underfunded and inadequate public sevices could be accompanied by a vision of a shabby hospital with a long waiting list). They should mobilise their pre-existing cognitive knowledge for example, recalling the four components of the free-market approach will be much easier if one knows roughly what such an approach is, without in any way having to be par-ticularly competent as an economist. And the interpreter must think logically, accompanying the speaker's own logic so as to reproduce it faithfully.

One last word on 'memory' is necessary in the context of analysis of a speech. There are two crucial moments in any speech, by definition. These are the be-ginning and the end. The consecutive interpreter must concentrate particularly hard on these and make sure they get them right.

The beginning is important as it is the point of departure for the 'journey' which any speech is. If someone – here, the interpreter – starts from the wrong point, they have little chance of following the right path or of arriving where they are supposed to.

The end is usually the most important part of a speech. The speaker has provided a description or a narration, or has argued a point, precisely because they wish to arrive at a given conclusion. If the interpreter follows the speaker most of the way along a speech but then misses the conclusion, it is highly likely that they will have missed the point of the speech. It may be that the conclusion is merely a recapitulation or a summary of what has gone before. All the better: that makes life easy for the interpreter. But that does not change the fact that it is crucial for the interpreter to provide that conclusion. It is also particularly important to insist on concentration at the end of a speech because the interpreter usually senses, instinctively, that this is the end, and because of that relaxes their attention. That is rather like an athlete who carelessly eases up after ninety-five metres of a one hundred metre race, only to be beaten at the tape. Rather than relaxing their attention, the interpreter must redouble their concentration at the end of a speech.

Re-expression

Having understood and analyzed, the consecutive interpreter must move on to re-expressing the speech they have just heard. Before discussing this, though, a parenthesis must be opened to deal with a possible intermediary phase. What if the interpreter, despite all their best efforts, has still not understood everything or is not in a position to reproduce it? They may have missed a number, a proper name. There may be a concept they need to have defined. There may be a part of an argument which is still obscure, perhaps through no fault of the interpreter, but simply because the speaker has not made themselves clear.

In all such circumstances it is perfectly legitimate for the interpreter to benefit from the fact that they are working in consecutive and put a question to the speaker. But there are a few basic rules to be followed in putting questions. First you must ask yourself whether the advantage of putting a question outweighs the disadvantage. For example, in a small technical working party it is fairly easy to ask questions without inconvenience. On the other hand, if the consecutive is the address of a visiting dignitary to an assembly of two hundred parliamentarians standing at a reception, it may well be better to resign oneself to an incomplete or imperfect consecutive and just get on with it.

Second, you must ask yourself in all honesty whether the question is really necessary to improve the interpretation, or whether it is just for your personal edification. Clearly, interpreters should not hold up proceedings out of pure intellectual curiosity.

Third, the interpreter should put their question, politely, to the speaker in the speaker's own language, and not forget to thank the speaker when the information is given.

There is, however, a fourth, more important consideration. The question, to be useful, must be clear and precise, and elicit an equally clear and precise answer from the speaker. One should not begin the question with something along the lines: 'I didn't understand...' or 'There was something I missed...', but rather with something which will not undermine the delegates' confidence in the interpreter, such as: 'Could you clarify...?'. Then, the question should be specific. If the problem is a number or a name, then the task is straightforward: one can ask, for example, 'Could you repeat the annual growth rate for steel exports?'. If a longer passage needs clarification the interpreter must situate the question for the speaker and ask for specific information. Let's assume a speaker has spent five minutes explaining the trade situation in relation to steel, and the interpreter is unsure about one point. Then it might be good to ask: 'When explaining why import tariffs on steel products should be increased you mentioned three factors. Could you remind me of the third factor?'. The worst kind of question would be: 'Somewhere towards the end you said something about steel imports I missed; could you repeat it?'. If the speaker is sensible they will refuse to answer the latter question. However, speakers often show goodwill and do their best to answer such vague questions, but then they have to repeat so much of the speech that it wastes time and fails to clarify the point the interpreter is interested in.

Lastly on this subject, when an interpreter has asked a question, they must concentrate particularly hard when listening to the answer and make sure they get it right in their interpretation. Nothing looks sillier than taking the trouble of asking a question but still missing the information out or getting it wrong.

Assuming now that the necessary clarifications have been given, the interpreter should have a speech which they have understood and analyzed. They now face the task of re-expressing. Given the way we have described the interpreter's role, it should be clear that they are not required to give an academically 'perfect' translation; they must not work in a solipsistic, introverted way. Simply, they must make sure the speaker is understood by the audience.

What does this mean in practice? First, in terms of presentation this means the interpreter must recognize they are a public speaker just like any other. They must establish contact with the audience, speaking up clearly and articulating. They must also establish eye contact with the audience. If they are working for just one client they should look at them regularly, though not stare fixedly at them. If they are working for a number of people they should look at the audience in general and look directly in turn at different members of the audience. The importance of eye contact has to be stressed particularly in that the consecutive interpreter will be working with the help of notes most of the time. They should avoid falling into the trap of looking at their notes all the time, either because they are deciphering enigmatic signs taken unclearly or because they are thinking hard about the meaning of the notes. On the contrary, the interpreter should glance down at their notes from time to time, just as an orator would look down at speaking notes, but have enough of the speech clear in their mind in order to be able to look at the audience most of the time.

The interpreter is called upon to deliver the speech efficiently. A speaker may hesitate, repeat themselves, choose long-winded ways of saying things. The interpreter, on the other hand, has heard everything and should know exactly what they want to say in the most efficient way the moment they open their mouth. This means the consecutive should only last about two-thirds to three-quarters of the time taken up by the original. The interpreter has to begin speaking practically as soon as the speaker has made it clear that they have finished (unless the interpreter needs to ask a question of the speaker), and then speak at a sustained, steady pace, without hesitation or unnecessary repetition. Here we say 'unnecessary' repetition because a speaker may deliberately use repetition as a rhetorical device which the interpreter needs to respect. Certainly, the interpreter should not introduce repetition which is not in the original by looking for just the right word, just the right turn of expression, and ending up offering the audience a number of versions of the same sentence with more or less synonymous words and expressions.

While saying that the interpreter must speak at a sustained, steady pace, we must also bear in mind the need to be sufficiently clear for the audience. This means the speed may be varied. For example, there may be parts of a speech where it is easy to follow the interpreter even if their delivery is rapid, but then elsewhere in the speech the interpreter provides, say, statistics they know delegates will want to note down: when providing the statistics the interpreter should slow down and articulate particularly clearly to make sure everything is audible.

In general terms the overall meaning of a speech may be brought out not just through the words used but also through the speaker's intonation and use of pauses. It is important for an interpreter to use these resources. In particular, just as sentences are separated by full stops on the written page, so sentences should be separated by the right use of the voice in interpretation: in many languages this means dropping one's voice at the end of the sentence and then making a short pause. Then again, as paragraphs can be indicated by indents in writing, a new paragraph, or section of a speech, may be indicated by a rather longer pause on the part of the interpreter. Use of such pauses may seem obvious, but it is an 'obvious' technique overlooked by some interpreters, whose technically correct translations lose much as they are presented in a monotonous, rather formless way.

Interpreting is a profession that is all about communication. This has important practical consequences for the content of the interpretation. In order to communicate well, the interpreter has to 'make their own speech' out of every speech they interpret. Yet they also have to be accurate and faithful to the speaker. How does the interpreter resolve this paradox?

The answer really lies in the understanding and analysis which have preceded the re-expression. The interpreter has understood in terms of ideas; they must therefore re-express in terms of ideas. The better their understanding and analysis, the better placed they are to express themselves freely, using their own words while respecting the content of the original. Provided the same ideas are being expressed, and the same relations between those ideas, the interpreter can invert the order of two sentences, merge two of the speaker's sentences into one of their own, or on the contrary divide one long sentence up into a number of shorter ones. They can replace a verbal expression with a substantival one: *After the President arrived* may become *After the President's arrival.* And so on. We will see later that the same reasoning applies to simultaneous interpreting, with similar results.

We have said the interpreter *can* re-express freely, but we should rather say that sometimes the interpreter *must* make such changes. A literal, word-for-word translation is not only undesirable, it is often impossible. The reasons for this may be purely mechanical, related to the grammar or lexis of different languages; they may also be due to different terms of cultural reference. Changes to the way ideas are expressed become ineluctable as one changes language, and, just as important, as one changes language culture.

The more the interpreter is in a position to express the speaker's ideas in their own words, the better will be the quality of communication between the speaker and the audience, the interpreter being merely a medium for that communication. This is surely the greatest paradox about the interpreter: the more creative the interpreter, the more they are faithful to the text; the more original they are – enhancing communication – the less obtrusive they are to the participants in a meeting! The best, most creative interpreters are the ones least noticed by their delegates.

In order to make a speech your own, as we said, you must have grasped it intellectually, fully understood and analyzed the ideas to be conveyed. But this is only half the battle.

One cannot overstate the importance of the interpreter's target-language skills. Just as their passive languages are never completely learned and they continue to work on them, so the interpreter must continue to work on their target language(s), even if the target language is their mother tongue. This means keeping abreast of recent developments in order to cope with modern terminology. But it also means constantly enriching your general vocabulary and attempting to improve your style through regular reading of a broad range of well-written publications. This is an activity, as well as following your own press, which is particularly important for interpreters living abroad, perhaps in no regular contact with any member of their own language community outside their professional activities, and whose mother tongue therefore runs the risk of becoming stilted or impoverished. To express ideas well, that is, efficiently, clearly and elegantly, one must have the richest possible resources available in the target language and be able to call on them whenever needed.

Exercises

Getting started on consecutive

1. Pre-consecutive exercises

(a) Make speeches of different types (narrative, logical argument, etc.; cf. comments above on speech types) and ask students:
   (i)   to identify the type of speech
   (ii) to analyze the structure of a speech
   (iii) to identify the main ideas and links between the ideas in any given speech.

Notes:
1) As these speeches are not to be interpreted they do not necessarily have to be linguistically and conceptually easy. Indeed, they should be sufficiently challenging to force students into attentive, active, analytical listening. They should be of about five to six minutes duration.

2)   The exercises mentioned above can be done in an open class discussion. This is preferable to asking one single student to do all the work for a given speech.

3)   To stress to the students that active listening and analysis are not *translation* exercises, such speeches can also be made for the students in their mother tongue and the discussion can be in the same language as the original speech.

(b)   Make speeches of different types and ask students individually to provide a résumé of them.

Notes:

1)   These speeches should be highly (indeed hyper-) structured to enable the students to analyze them clearly and provide a satisfactory résumé.

2)   The speeches should not be too linguistically complex: dealing with language problems is not part of this exercise.

3)   The speech may be of three to maximum five minutes duration.

4)   The trainer should insist on the résumé genuinely being one: e.g. a five-minute argumentative speech with introduction, three argumentative paragraphs and a conclusion should be summarized in no more than five sentences.

5)   As for (a) above, such exercises can be (but do not have to be) done monolingually, preferably from the students' mother tongue into the same.

2. Consecutive exercises

By 'consecutive exercises' we mean quite simply students doing consecutive interpreting. First consecutive exercises should be done without the students having the possibility of taking notes (so-called 'memory exercises'). Accordingly, speeches should contain few or no numbers and other elements difficult to remember without notes.

The very first speeches should be linguistically and conceptually easy and last about three minutes. Working toward the introduction of note-taking, the complexity of speeches may be gradually increased and their duration increased to about five minutes.

Students should begin by working into their mother tongue.

Sometimes such consecutive exercises may be done monolingually, again to stress to students that there is more to the exercise than the problem of translation from one language to another.

3. Note-taking in Consecutive Interpreting

A number of readers may be annoyed that the above discussion of the basic principles of consecutive has been carried out to a large extent as if notes did not exist. One may have gleaned the impression that the interpreter was to analyze and memorize speeches of up to five minutes without any real assistance from notes. It is obvious that none but exceptional interpreters can be expected to work in that way: our presentation in the previous chapter was merely designed to put note-taking in the right perspective.

The essential part of a consecutive interpreter's work is done in the activities already described: understanding, analysis, re-expression. If these are not done correctly, the best notes in the world will not make you a good interpreter. Notes are no more than an aid to enhance the work done on the basis of these three key components. They are not an end in themselves, but a means to an end.

The interpreter who invests too much in their notes is running a twofold risk. First, by trying to note as much as possible in a form as close as possible to the original, their notes may become a form of shorthand, a mere transcription of the sequence of words used by the speaker. Such notes will influence the interpreter when they are reproducing the speech, and their version will be too much a transliteration of the original, not a re-expression of its ideas.

Second, and more seriously, the interpreter who relies too much on their notes will have paid insufficient attention to genuine understanding and analysis while listening to the speech. They are therefore capable of being superficial, of making serious errors, even of contradicting themselves, insofar as the speech for them is no longer a coherent whole but a series of sentences to be reproduced automatically. They are, so to speak, flying blind.

Having sounded these warning notes about the attitude to take to notes, and the risks involved in their abuse, what then is the purpose of taking notes?

The first and most obvious use of notes is to relieve memory. However well the interpreter may analyze a speech and order its ideas with a view to their recall (interpreter's 'memory'), there will still be too many elements in a five-minute speech for an interpreter to recall everything. This is particularly true if a speech contains numbers, names, lists and so on, since such elements cannot be recalled on the basis of analysis and logic. Further, if the interpreter devotes their intellectual energies to remembering, say, a list of chemicals, this may distract them from the key task of listening attentively to what comes next. By noting things in such a way that they know when and how they fit into the speech, the interpreter need not burden their memory with such information; they can continue to devote their mental faculties to listening actively to the rest of the speech. Bear in mind that an interpreter is rarely called upon to interpret just one speech: if you are working intensively in consecutive for a session of three hours it is crucial to reduce fatigue by relieving your memory through notes.

The second purpose of notes is what we should call 'jogging' the interpreter's memory. The term 'relieving' memory was used to cover noting down specific elements so the interpreter can reproduce the *content* of a speech. But notes can also be used to enhance the interpreter's ability to reproduce the *structure* of a speech. Notes should therefore reflect the form of a speech, making it clear to the interpreter what is important and what is ancillary, how ideas are related or separated from one another. This structure should also be in the interpreter's mind; it should be the product of their analytical work. Pinning the structure down in notes can be helpful in two ways. First, having to reflect the structure in notes can function as a kind of discipline, forcing the interpreter to make the analysis. Second, if the structure is already on the page, when it comes to reproducing the speech the written structure can 'jog' the interpreter's memory, making it easier to verbalize the desired structure.

Practical Points for Note-taking

Note-taking is among other things a mechanical exercise, and a number of purely practical indications should be followed. An interpreter must be able to take their notes quickly and write upon something convenient to hold and easy to handle. We would recommend a stenographer's note-pad, roughly 15cm by 20cm. Loose sheets of paper should definitely be avoided, as they may become disordered. For any given speech the interpreter should write on only the recto side of successive pages of the note-pad. It is too awkward to write on both sides, recto-verso, while taking notes, and if you do, there is the risk that you might lose sight of the order in which notes were taken. It is easier just to keep flipping the pages over always in the same direction. To write with, one should have something reliable that flows quickly across the page; the best thing is probably still the good old-fashioned lead pencil.

It is primordial that the interpreter's notes should be easily legible. Under 're-expression' above we stressed the need for the interpreter to communicate, which involves the appropriate body language and eye contact with delegates. Therefore, the interpreter cannot afford to have notes that they have to decipher as they go along. The meaning the interpreter wishes to express should leap up at them from the page. This means the interpreter should write in large characters. Further, notes should be well spread out over the page so that the various elements can be clearly differentiated. The combination of these two points means that interpreters find themselves getting through a lot of paper, perhaps noting just one sentence on a page of the note-pad: they should have no qualms about this. Note also that the interpreter's notes must be totally unequivocal. For example, *ind* cannot be used as an abbreviation on the one hand for *industrial* and elsewhere for *independent*. Such ambiguity will at best make for a less efficient reading of notes, and at worst lead to silly mistakes. If an interpreter wishes to use symbols or abbreviations, they should not succumb to the temptation of inventing them in the course of a speech in a way which does not make immediate and glaring sense. If a new symbol is used, it should be so obvious as to be unproblematic.

What to Note

The things to be noted are quite logically related to the analysis of the speech, as described in the relevant section above. The first things to be noted should thus be the main ideas. One could argue that because these are the main ideas they will be remembered anyway, so there is no need noting them. However, the notes used for the main ideas are not so much there to help the interpreter remember as to provide a skeleton outline of the speech. Proceeding on the basis of the subject-verb-object analysis described above, the interpreter will then be able to find in their notes the sequence of ideas constituting the speech. This should help the interpreter reproduce the speech without faltering, moving swiftly from one idea to the next without having to search in their mind for the next idea. The notes here are not so much a record of each idea in detail as a prompt to cue the interpreter as they finish one idea and wish to start the next one.

Then, just as in the mental analysis of a speech one has to identify the links and separations between ideas, so these links and separations should appear in the notes. It may well be that the speech has such a clear logic that the interpreter can fill in the links without having to note them, but most of the time the situation is not so clear, and it is absolutely crucial to render links correctly, as demonstrated in the previous chapter. Indeed, if anything, the links are rather more important to note than the so-called 'main ideas' themselves. An important idea, provided it has impressed itself clearly on the interpreter's mind, either through visualization or because it is a clear abstract idea, can easily be noted in a very abbreviated form, perhaps even by one keyword. If a British delegate complains, 'Ships from the Spanish fishing fleet have been fishing illegally in British waters', in the context of a given meeting it may well be possible for the interpreter to note this as *Spanish fishers!* and to rely on their memory for the rest. On the other hand, it may not be so easy to deal with links such as *but*, *therefore*, *since* and so on without noting them. It is thus very advisable to note links systematically. Where there should be a clear separation between ideas ('zero link'), this should also be clearly shown in notes.

A third element that should always be part of an interpreter's analysis of a speech, and which should also appear in the notes, is the point of view being expressed. The same arguments apply here as to links: it is important to reflect points of view in an interpretation and it may not always be easy to build these in faithfully without some reminder from notes.

Fourth, we have already noted that delegates need to know 'what happened when', and that the tenses of verbs are therefore important. When noting verbs, interpreters should thus take care to note the tense correctly, and if appropriate the mode, in particular the conditional. Similarly, it is a good idea to note modal verbs. Modal verbs have a decisive influence on the function of other verbs and determine the meaning of a sentence.

All of the points mentioned so far are elements that fit into the intellectual analysis of a speech by the interpreter; they are thus to be noted as a kind of insurance policy. The interpreter could conceivably remember all the main ideas without notes, with the links between them and the points of view reflected in the original. But the notes are there to jog the memory by reflecting the structure of the speech, to ensure efficiency and completeness in delivery, and to ensure faithfulness to the original particularly with respect to links and points of view.

However, there are also elements that an interpreter cannot remember or does not want to make the effort to remember, and where notes are used to relieve memory. The first of these is numbers. Numbers are totally abstract, and any but the simplest numbers become difficult to retain in one's mind for five minutes or so. Once a series of numbers is cited, notes become indispensable. Dates are to be considered in the same light. Numbers may be spoken very quickly by a speaker, particularly if there is a series of numbers to be given. It is important for the interpreter to note them all, so when an interpreter realizes that numbers are going to be given, or if they hear a number, they should drop everything else and note it immediately. If the interpreter hesitates about noting the number, finishing off noting the previous sentence, or the introduction to the number, there is a serious risk they will never get the number. If the speaker gives a series of numbers, the problem is clearly even worse. But if the interpreter gives priority to the numbers, it will be possible for the interpreter to jot them down and then return to tidying up the note-taking of the previous idea, which it will be easier to retain in their mind.

For example, take the following extract of a speech:

> Our exports to our European partners have progressed well over the last year, although we have had more difficulty in exporting to countries with weaker currencies, who had sometimes deliberately made competitive devaluations in order to achieve a trade advantage through undervaluation of their currency. For example, exports to Germany progressed by 3.2%, to $25.7 million, whereas in the case of Italy export growth was a marginal 0.6%, total exports amounting to $11.4 million.

The first sentence expresses a coherent, logical notion, which it is relatively easy to recall. Let's assume that the interpreter has got as far as noting *competitive devaluations*, when the speaker says *For example*. There, the interpreter should sense that numbers are coming; they should stop noting the previous sentence in order to be sure to note the figures correctly. Once the figures are noted the interpreter can quickly tidy up the end of the previous sentence, which they will have held latent in their memory while concentrating on the figures.

Second, there are proper names. You might be able to retain well-known and familiar names, but once a few are mentioned or if the interpreter is not well acquainted with a name, notes are essential. Bear in mind that a proper name in a speech usually has a certain intrinsic importance. Moreover, proper names are not limited to people's names: they may also be geographical names, or names of companies or organizations, perhaps expressed as acronyms. To make matters worse, not only might the interpreter be unfamiliar with a name, they may have no idea of how the name is written. Indeed, the name may be written in a script unfamiliar to the interpreter (a Chinese or Japanese name for a European interpreter possessing neither of those two languages, for example). In such cases, the interpreter should ignore orthography, remembering that notes are there only for them, as a means to an end. They should note down phonetically and as closely as possible what they believe they have heard. The worst-case scenario is when the speaker doesn't really know how to pronounce the name either, and mangles it. Then there are two possibilities. Either the interpreter is no wiser than the speaker, in which case they can do little more than note down what they have heard, and then reproduce it to the best of their ability afterwards. Or the interpreter can identify the speaker's mistake and deduce what they were trying to say, in which case they can note the name as it suits them and produce the correct pronunciation in their interpretation.

Lastly, lists should always be noted as completely as possible. All too often when a speaker arrives at a list, be it of chemicals, agricultural products, fish or whatever, they reel off the items at great speed. The interpreter should note the elements as completely as possible, as otherwise they have little chance of remembering them. This means they should stop noting everything else once they realize the speaker is about to give a list or has just begun one. The interpreter should use the same technique as with numbers. If the list is given too quickly for them to note down everything, they should note clearly that something is missing; if more than one element is missing they should note how many. When the speaker has finished they can then assess whether they wish the list to be repeated. Thus, if a speaker says at speed, 'The countries concerned are Venezuela, Colombia, Peru, Bolivia, Panama and Cuba', and the interpreter misses the second and fifth names, they can note:

Venezuela

–

Peru
Bolivia

–

Cuba.

This will enable the interpreter to put their question correctly to the speaker afterwards.

To sum up, the interpreter's notes should give at least the main ideas of a speech with the links between those ideas; points of view, tenses of verbs, and modal verbs, should also be noted; to relieve their memory, the interpreter should note numbers, dates, names and lists. These are the bare requirements of notes. Interpreters may of course choose to note much more. Some colleagues have highly efficient note-taking techniques that enable them to take down practically everything. Others prefer to write absolutely the strict minimum and rely for the rest on their intellect and memory. Both approaches are defensible. Note-taking is very much a question of personal taste. The one thing to be avoided, we repeat, is trying to note everything down as an end in itself, to the detriment of the interpreter's active listening to the original.

How to Note

Diagonal Layout

We have stressed that notes should reflect the structure of a speech clearly so as to help the interpreter reproduce that structure in their interpretation. But how is this actually done in practice?

We have already said that the main ideas based around a subject-verb-object analysis should be noted. To reflect this analysis on the page, the interpreter should separate the three components quite clearly and allocate to each of them roughly the same position in any given section of notes. These positions will form a diagonal axis, working from left to right of a page and from top to bottom, thus:

subject

verb

object

A number of ideas may be contained on one page, the beginning of each one being clearly marked by the move back to the left-hand side of the page. The interpreter is of course not limited to noting just the subject, verb and object, but it is around this basic structure that they will be able to build in other details in the notes if they desire (cf. above, 'what to note').

This diagonal presentation has become something of an article of faith since Rozan's epoch-making book on note-taking *La prise de notes en interprétation consécutive* (1956), where it was called *décalage* ('shift'). But Rozan himself gives relatively little explanation as to why he recommends it, and one may quite justifiably ask why diagonal presentation should be preferred. There are several reasons. First, the diagonal layout forces the interpreter to separate components of a sentence on a page in a way which avoids all confusion. Clearly separated and distinct notes are important for ease of reading. Second, as just mentioned, the beginning of each new idea is clearly marked. Third, notes must be taken in a concise and non-literary manner. The great temptation is to take notes horizontally and then to align ideas one above another.

For example, let us take :

> Hungary has complained that its steel exports to the European Union are unable to develop because of excessively restrictive tariff quotas. But the Union representative pointed out that quotas are still underused by Hungary by a large margin, so the tariff quotas themselves didn't appear to be creating the difficulties.

This could be noted:

> HU complained – steel exports to EU can't develop
> Because too strict tariff quotas
> But EU rep – quotas underused by HU a lot
> So quotas not prob

The drawbacks here become immediately apparent. The interpreter, taking notes rather as a meeting secretary or a student at a university lecture, is writing too much. The ideas do not stand out clearly at a glance from the page. And the ideas are not analyzed through the notes (even though they may be in the interpreter's mind): they are a slavish reproduction of the words used by the speaker, in the order in which they were spoken, which will tend to lead the interpreter to function similarly when actually reproducing the speech orally. The upshot will probably be an unanalyzed interpretation with inferior style, as the expression in the target language will be too influenced by the form of expression in the source language.

The diagonal form offers a natural movement for one's eyes to move from left to right and from top to bottom of a page when reading. By combining these two natural movements and reproducing them in the diagonal layout the interpreter will make it easier for themselves to pick out the elements of a sentence as they cast their eyes rapidly over a page. Of course, this last comment only applies to users of script which is read from left to right and from top to bottom. Interpreters of Chinese, Japanese and Arabic, for example, must adapt their note-taking systems as they see fit.

The Left-hand Margin

The second major component of a speech which we have said should be reflected in notes are the links between ideas and the separations between ideas. The links lie, by definition, outside the subject-verb-object presentation, so a special place has to be found for them. Given that the diagonal layout involves bringing your eyes back to the left-hand side of the page to start a new idea, the logical place to put the link is to the extreme left of the page, just before the beginning of the substantive idea. To make sure that links are easy to find, and to avoid any confusion with the subject of the sentence a link introduces, it is best to leave a left-hand margin of one to two centimetres for links. Some interpreters may choose to draw a margin down the left-hand side of the page; others may choose merely to keep the margin notional. The link is noted at the same level on the page as the subject of the sentence it is introducing. Thus, if we take the example: 'Grain exports to the United States have been unable to develop because the United States have imposed high import tariffs', this could be noted :

$$\text{Grain exports}$$
$$\text{unable develop}$$
$$\text{to US}$$
$$\text{because US}$$
$$\text{imposed}$$
$$\text{high tariffs}$$

(This example serves merely to show the structure of notes: no interpreter would seriously note long-hand in this way.) The first idea is easily identifiable in the diagonal layout; the link stands out clearly in the left-hand margin; and the second idea follows from it equally clearly.

Besides being used for links, the left-hand column is also ideal for representing points of view, another key element in notes. To show this we return to the text used above for the example of unwanted horizontal note-taking:

> Hungary has complained that its steel exports to the European Union are not able to develop because of excessively restrictive tariff quotas. But the Union representative pointed out that quotas are still underused by Hungary by a large margin, so the tariff quotas themselves didn't appear to be creating the difficulties.

This could now be noted:

HU : steel exports

             cannot develop

                      to EU

because tariff quotas

            too restrictive

          ——————

but EU : HU

         underuses a lot

                 quotas

so   quotas

       not problem.

From this example one can see how links and points of view can be easily picked out by the interpreter. They can even be combined, as in *but EU*. Here the economy of note-taking for points of view becomes apparent. Hungary *complained*, the EU representative *pointed out*, but these words as such do not need to be noted: the interpreter will remember the first verb with the help of the context, and the second verb could just as well have been *said*, *stated*, or any of a number of equivalents.

Before leaving the question of the left-hand margin we should recall that ideas do not just need to be linked, but on occasions they need to be separated. It may therefore be very useful to draw a short line after each idea to separate it clearly from the next one. If this is considered superfluous, as the diagonal layout of a page should in any case separate ideas, a line should at least be drawn after each complete sentence. Thus, in the example above one could draw a line after *too restrictive*, and, assuming the speech continues, after *not problem*. In any case, clear separations should be made between different paragraphs or sections of a speech. This can be done, for example, by drawing a line across the entire width of the page, rather than a short one as for separation of ideas; alternatively one may draw three short, vertical lines in the left-hand margin before a new paragraph or section, to symbolize a paragraph indent. The way the separation is made is unimportant, provided it is perfectly clear to the interpreter, who then has to read back their own notes.

Verticality of Lists

An exception to the general principle of diagonal layout is that lists should be noted vertically. The elements in the list have the same value and should therefore be attributed the same position in notes. Thus, one could note 'Western Turkey has suffered a series of natural catastrophes, violent winter storms, flooding and earthquake' as:

W. TY

suffered

catas : storms
          floods
          earthquakes

A list can of course occur anywhere in a sentence. It may equally well affect the subject or the verb. For example, the previous sentence could have begun, 'European Turkey, north-east Greece and southern Bulgaria have all suffered...', in which case one would note:

Eur TY
NE Greece
S Bulg

suffered ...

If I've Missed Something Out in My Notes

It will happen to all interpreters some time in their career that they fail to hear something, or hearing it fail to register it immediately, and so are unable to note it down, while knowing that there is something they have missed. In those circumstances, you will want to put a question to the speaker afterwards, and to put the question you will want to know where the relevant point in the speech is and what its context is. This means you should note clearly that something is missing. The simplest thing is to put a very large cross in the right-hand margin of the notes at the same level as the missing item would have been in the notes. This will enable you to find the point on that page. But the interpreter also needs to be able to find the relevant page, and quickly, so as not to keep delegates waiting while they look for their question. An easy thing to do is to have a spare pencil or pen available, and to slip it in between the pages of your notepad at the page relevant to the question. This will make it possible at the end of a speech to flip back immediately to the passage concerned and put your question quickly and directly.

Abbreviations and Symbols

The obvious advantage of abbreviations and symbols is that they help save time in taking notes, thus adding to the efficiency of note-taking. Further, by reducing an idea, which may be expressed by one word or a number of words, to a symbol, the interpreter finds it easier to escape the trap of word-for-word translation. The symbol represents an idea, rather than the word or words, and the interpreter, seeing the symbol in their notes, is more liable to think in terms of the idea rather than of words.

Having decided that one wishes to use abbreviations and symbols, the question immediately arises as to what extent they should be used. One could take the minimalist view of use of symbols as being represented by Rozan, who in his *Prise de notes* states that one can make do with 20 symbols and that of these in fact only ten are indispensable. Other schools of thought have tended to a maximalist approach, developing comprehensive systems of symbolization such as that taught for a number of years by Matyssek at Heidelberg, enshrined in his 1989 *Handbuch der Notizentechnik für Dolmetscher.*

As in so many areas of interpretation we would argue that the approach you adopt is very much a question of personal taste. Both the minimalist and the maximalist positions, and indeed any other intermediary station, have their merits. Rather than laying down a hard-and-fast rule as to the desirable degree of symbolization, it is better to let each interpreter find their own balance. But in trying to strike that balance a number of basic principles should be observed.

First, it should be remembered that abbreviations and symbols are, like any other part of notes, a means to an end, and not an end in themselves. There is little point in creating a vast, perhaps intellectually satisfying, system of abbreviations and symbols if the system does not help the interpreter to interpret better. For the interpreter to benefit fully from note-taking, their abbreviations and symbols must be unequivocal. It must be immediately obvious to the interpreter reading back their notes exactly what all their abbreviations and symbols mean.

This pleads against the arbitrary creation of complex, abstract systems that the interpreter will have difficulty manipulating and remembering. Such a system may prevent the interpreter from listening attentively and analyzing the original, as they concentrate on the purely technical question of how to transform the speaker's words into symbols. Worse, even assuming the interpreter has noted correctly, they may then have difficulty in reading back their notes. Of course, this does not mean that an interpreter cannot evolve an extensive system of abbreviations and symbols. The simple condition is that they should always be perfectly clear and make sense to the interpreter.

To make sense, abbreviations and symbols must be 'logical' to the interpreter using them. The word 'logical' is deliberately placed in inverted commas here, in that we mean that abbreviations and symbols should have an intrinsic connotative function for the interpreter who uses them. That is, they should be genuinely symbols, not just signs. But as the interpreter is the creator of their own symbols, the person who writes them and the only person who needs to read them, the only 'logic' they need to respect is that the abbreviations and symbols they use should 'logically' mean something to them. It may well be that the symbols of one interpreter are meaningless or illogical to any other interpreter, but that is neither here nor there. For example, one interpreter may find that a schematic pitchfork, looking like the Greek letter *psi*, means agriculture. The resemblance with the pitchfork makes this symbol logical for that interpreter, even if for another one the Greek letter means something else, or maybe nothing at all.

If a symbol is meaningful to the interpreter who uses it, the symbol should stand a good chance of becoming 'organic' in the sense that other symbols can be derived from it by using the same subjective logic. Thus, an interpreter may wish to use *?* to indicate *demand* in the economic sense of 'supply and demand', as a question mark triggers in their mind the notion of asking, and thus demand. They may then take the inverse of *?*, which is), to indicate 'supply' in the same economic context. Clearly, there is no way that) can logically mean 'supply' if one does not know the genesis of this symbol, but in this case it has grown organically, so to speak, out of another symbol.

In summary, then, abbreviations and symbols are very much a personal affair. They are indispensable and can well afford to go beyond the very modest limits laid down by Rozan. But interpreters should not impose on themselves the straitjacket of an arbitrary system which they then try to learn by rote as they would mathematical formulas. Abbreviations and symbols must be unequivocal, logical to their user, and form an organic system.

Having stated these basic principles, we can now look in more detail at the way abbreviations and symbols can be used.

Frequently Occurring Notions

Any notion that is likely to occur often in an interpreter's work should have its corresponding abbreviation or symbol. Such abbreviations and symbols will necessarily save much effort and should not be difficult to remember insofar as they will be in constant use. Practically all interpreters, as they work in an international context, should have a list of abbreviations for the country names they come across most frequently. Here an easy solution is to take international car registration codes, or the first letter of the country name, or some mix of these. As always in notes, all ambiguity is to be avoided: *CH* is fine for Switzerland, provided there is something different for China, and so on. Similarly, interpreters should have something to represent the major international organizations. As a general rule these are designated by acronyms, which the interpreter can just copy, but there are one or two others, such as the World Bank, where a specific abbreviation may come in handy.

Beyond this common core, each interpreter should have abbreviations or symbols for the notions that come up frequently in their own particular area. This will obviously concern the content of meetings: someone working regularly for trades unions may want symbols for *collective bargaining* or *collective bargaining agreement*, which will not be a vast amount of use to, say, a staff interpreter at NATO. Such frequently occurring notions often concern not the substantive content of discussions but rather the apparatus and general procedural environment of the organisations interpreters work for. European Union interpreters should have a symbol or abbreviation for each of the institutions of the Union, for *Presidency of the Council*, for the main policy instruments and funds of the Union, and so on; United Nations interpreters should have something for *General Assembly, resolution, Security Council*, perhaps even *permanent member of the Security Council*.

Then there is the whole range of notions which may occur often enough for an interpreter to decide it is worthwhile having a symbol or abbreviation systematically for them. Words such as *political, economic, budgetary, monetary, industry, agriculture, territory, country, international* (the list is literally endless) and all their derivatives. Each interpreter is free to choose whether or not to use abbreviations and symbols for these, but if they do so they should respect the general principles mentioned above, namely that the symbols be intrinsically meaningful to them, and can thus be developed organically. One way of creating an inner logic in symbols, and at the same time making them easier to remember, is to take them in groups. Thus, for example, one may decide that *economic, monetary, budgetary* and *financial* are four words justifying a symbol, and that as they are related but distinct notions they should be represented by related but carefully differentiated symbols. These symbols could be the first letter of each word transcribed into the Greek alphabet, thus being respectively ε, μ, β, φ. These symbols can in turn be developed by being combined with others. Then, if *increase, improvement* is noted by using ↑, *growth* in the sense of 'economic growth' could be noted ε↑; a budget surplus could be noted β+; and so on. Thus, by using family groups of symbols and logical combinations of symbols, a vast range of frequently occurring notions can be noted without being a burden to the interpreter either when they are noting or when they are reading back their notes.

However, a note of warning should be sounded here. In creating family groups of symbols the interpreter has the freedom to link ideas without being tied down by words. But they must then use their symbols with total rigour in order to avoid vagueness and confusion. If the sign G is used to mean 'country', then Gal can mean 'national'. The interpreter can ignore that lexically *national* is derived from *nation*, and the interpreter may choose to symbolize *country* rather than *nation*, as it is a more frequently used notion. But then, if *nation* is used by a speaker, what does the interpreter do in their note-taking? Some might argue that they can still use the symbol G and just remember that on this occasion the word is different. We would argue, however, that this means taking an immense risk; it is opening the door to the possibility of confusing *country* and *nation*, two notions that it may be necessary to distinguish. And if the one symbol can do for *country* and *nation*, why not for *state*? Then where does the interpreter stand if the debate turns to the question of the *nation-state*? Here the limits of symbolization become clear. Either the interpreter writes the adjacent notions of 'nation' and 'state' long-hand or in some abbreviated form, or they choose different symbols for them. We thus condone family groups of symbols, but not fudging or the ambiguous multivalence of individual symbols within a family.

Lastly, we should mention notions that occur frequently only in the context of a given meeting. For these, ad hoc symbols and abbreviations can be devised. For example, let's assume that in a meeting on regional development, the phrase *town and country planning* is mentioned repeatedly. This is not the kind of notion you normally have a symbol up your sleeve for. But nothing prevents the interpreter from noting it as TCP. This abbreviation serves its purpose during the meeting and will be forgotten the next day. The following week the same interpreter may be in a meeting where the *Transport Combination Programme* lies at the heart of the debate. This too can become TCP. In neither case is there a risk of confusion for the interpreter. In another meeting *local authorities, regional authorities* and *national authorities* are key terms. These can be abbreviated to LA, RA and NA, even if, for example, the interpreter has a different symbol they habitually use for *national* which could have been brought in here. The context and the convenience of using a group of ad hoc abbreviations make NA the obvious thing to note for *national authorities,* thus actually overriding the interpreter's existing note-taking conventions.

Links

Links, it has already been said, are to be noted systematically. To do so accurately, quickly and efficiently, it is best to have some very short form for all links. These short forms do not have to be symbols, nor even abbreviations. There are a number of very short link words in English which can be used as they stand: *as* for anything in the 'because' family; *but* for all words and phrases of that family, including 'however' and 'on the other hand'; and *so* for anything in the 'therefore' family. Interpreters into languages other than English can use these English words in their notes, even if essentially they take notes in the target language: there is no reason why interpreters should not borrow convenient short words from other languages for their notes.

Alternatively, you may use the mathematical sign ∴ to mean 'therefore', and, if you desire, the same sign inverted to mean 'because'. Or again, some interpreters may prefer to express causality using arrows, such that ⇒ means 'therefore' and ⇐ means 'because', for example (although we will have more to say below on arrows). Whatever the solution, the links must be clear and easy to note quickly.

Similarly, points of view should be easy to note, in particular the notions of 'saying' something and 'thinking' something. The symbols or abbreviations used to reflect these notions are not limited to those two verbs, and can cover a wide range of expressions. 'To say' may reflect announcing, declaring, and so on. One may even wish to use it in notes where there is no real utterance, for example when a report 'says' that.... Likewise, 'to think' may be used to note feeling, being of the opinion that, etc. For all such indications of subjectivity, two symbols suffice, perhaps " for 'to say' and ≡ for 'to think'.

Tenses

The tenses that are most important to note are the present, the past and the future. It is barely useful to differentiate in notes between different past tenses, such as an imperfect and a past perfect: such differences often fail to transfer directly between two languages, and in any case the appropriate tense will probably be used instinctively by the interpreter. It may be possible to note tenses by using short words such as *will* and *has* in English. However, if you use this technique the words used should be considered as signs, not as words used according to the rules of grammar. They should not, therefore, be conjugated. Even so, noting tenses in this way may tempt interpreters into a too literal and too horizontal note-taking technique. Moreover, for languages where a future or a past is indicated by verb endings to the stem, interpreters may find such an approach inconvenient or unnatural.

A second option would be to add suffixes to verbs such as *-ed* for the past and *-ll* for the future. The grounds for this are that the regular English past tense is formed by the suffix *-ed* and in spoken English a future may be expressed by the suffix *-'ll*. If you are noting in a language other than English you can choose to borrow the English suffixes or use other ones arising naturally from the target language.

There is, however, a third option, which has the advantage of being totally symbolic, since it is a graphic presentation of tense and thus totally independent of language. You can use the idea that what is past is 'backward-looking', which can be symbolized by the sign ⌋ ; contrariwise, the future can be ⌊; and the present can be indicated by default. Thus, 'is opposing' is noted simply *oppose*; 'opposed' can be *oppose*⌋ or ⌋ *oppose*; and 'will oppose' can be ⌊*oppose* or *oppose*⌊. The length of the horizontal line is up to the individual interpreter, as is the question as to whether to put the symbol before or after the verb stem.

You may find that this does not necessarily save time in note-taking, as compared with suffixes, or even writing the verb long-hand, as in *opposed*. Sometimes this will be true. But the real advantage of noting tenses in this symbolic way is that the interpreter can immediately recognize the tense when reading back their notes. You don't have to bother with noting irregular past or future tenses, and you don't have to care about sequence of tenses in languages where that is relevant: the correct form of expression will be provided by the interpreter in their oral rendering but does not need to be present in the notes.

If an interpreter wishes to note a pluperfect they can do so by using the 'past' symbol, but double underlining, so as to indicate a further remove in time, thus: ⌊.

It may also be useful to indicate the conditional or subjunctive modes, depending on the target language. The symbol chosen for this and its place in relation to the verb can be chosen freely by each interpreter, provided it is clear. One widely-used option is to place a circumflex accent over the verb. Thus, 'would oppose' becomes *oppose*.

Modal verbs

Again, it is a moot point as to whether symbols or abbreviations are necessary or even desirable for modal verbs. Since these are verbs that occur frequently and are intrinsically important in most languages, interpreters might feel it is worthwhile having symbols. On the other hand, modals tend to be short words

– *can*, *must*, *want*, etc., and not just in English – , and one may get by without anything special for them.

That said, we would argue that it is probably better to have symbols for modals, for two reasons. First, notions expressed by modals can also be expressed in a number of other ways, and it will be useful to have a single simple symbol to which one can reduce all such forms of expression. Thus, if 'must' is symbolized as Δ, then wording such as 'will be obliged to' can be noted as Δ⌊.

Second, modals can have more than one meaning, and sometimes where there is just one modal in one language it can be translated with two different modals in an other language. For example, the English *can* can mean 'to be (physically) capable of, to know how to', and also 'to be allowed to, to have permission to'. In a number of languages these two senses are reflected by different verbs. By symbolizing modals the interpreter is more likely to pinpoint the correct notion in their notes and will run less of a risk of being trapped by the ambivalence of the modal in the source language, and thus of mistranslating.

If one does choose to use symbols for modal verbs it is best to treat them as a family group and develop an organically related set of symbols to represent them.

Stress

Speakers inevitably qualify their comments by stressing particular points or words, or, alternatively, by attenuating them. In order to be able to render all shades of meaning it is a good thing for an interpreter to note such qualifications. This can be done very simply through a system of underlining. For example, if something is said to be 'very important', this can be noted as *important*. If the interpreter wants they can extend the system by noting 'extremely important' using double underlining. On the other hand, 'fairly important' could be noted by underlining, but using a squiggly line. This, or any similar simple system, may make it easy to note a whole range of nuances with great ease.

Interpreters may also wish to abbreviate the way they note comparatives and superlatives. They may use suffixes such as *-er* and *-st*, inspired from the standard English suffixes. Again this is possible even if the notes are in a different language. Alternatively, you may prefer to use a symbol such as + for comparison, with ++ for superlative; or > for comparative ('more than'), in which case < can be used for 'less', and so on. The choice is up to the individual interpreter. The key thing is that the system should be consistent and unequivocal.

Arrows

Arrows are particularly useful tools in a graphic system of note-taking. The sense of the arrow will have an intrinsic meaning, obvious in context. Thus ↑ will mean increase (quantitatively) and improvement (qualitatively); ↓ will mean the opposite. Such signs can be used in combination with others, as mentioned above. For example, if ε is 'economy', ε↑ is 'economic growth'. The position of an arrow in relation to the words or other symbols noted can also be significant. 'Unemployment continues to be at a high level' can quite simply be noted as:

unemployment ⁻⁾

The arrow itself signifies 'continues to be', and the fact that the arrow is 'high' above the word it qualifies indicates the level of unemployment.

Arrows can be made oblique and used to express trends or progressive change. Thus *inflation* ___| may mean 'inflation has tended to increase'. Interpreters may refine the system further and draw arrows with a straight line in normal circumstances, but with a squiggly line if a notion has been attenuated. Then 'inflation has tended to increase slightly' could become *inflation* ___|.

Arrows can also signify simply movement : 'US car exports to Japan' could be noted *US cars → J*. They can be two-way (↔) to indicate reciprocity. They can be double-headed (⇐, ⇔, ⇒) for special meanings. They can be in any direction one wants to represent things graphically. For example, if μ is 'money, currency', then the entire phrase 'serious exchange-rate fluctuations' can be noted μ_____ . The sinuous line tells us the currency is going up and down, i.e. the exchange rate is fluctuating, and the underlining tells us it is serious.

Finally, some interpreters may choose to use arrows to indicate logical links, in particular causality as mentioned above.

The use of arrows therefore opens up a whole range of expression to the interpreter. The potential is practically unlimited. However, we must stress, as in all other areas of notes, that the interpreter must know exactly what their own symbols mean, and should not use arrows which have ambiguous meanings. If a particular type of arrow, say ⇒, is used to indicate causality, it should not also be used to indicate geographical movement or progression in time.

Besides arrows interpreters may wish to use lines without arrow-heads at all. This may be done to express meaning directly. In the example 'serious exchange-rate fluctuations', one can argue that the arrow-head does not make the symbolization any clearer, and that μ followed by a kind of sine wave would be sufficient to note the idea. Further, there is a much more general and useful way of using lines. It will often happen that you want to note the same notion more than once on the same page. Rather than note twice, you can draw a line from the place where it is noted for the first time to the place where one would ordinarily note it for the second time, but then you leave that space empty in the notes. This technique, rather like dragging an icon from one place to another on a computer screen, is particularly useful if the notion noted cannot be symbolized or abbreviated simply. Take the text

> 'Town and country planning has become more and more a topic for consideration at European level. That is why the European Commission wishes to launch a vast European debate on town and country planning.'

This could be noted:

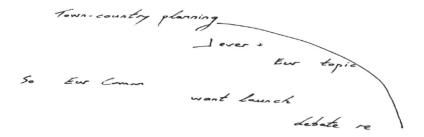

These notes are purely an example; they could be done any number of other ways, but here they show clearly the energy and time saving by simply dragging an element down to another place on the page with one line.

Suffixes

We have already insisted that symbols and abbreviations should not be ambiguous: *ind* cannot mean both 'industry' and 'independent' just as *diff* cannot mean 'different' and 'difficult', and so on. When you are using abbreviations, a way of differentiating words is to use suffixes. In languages where there are standard suffixes – such as *-ation*, *-ing* or *-ment* in English – this is easy to do, and it has the added advantage of gathering together words into family groups. Thus, one could note *prod* for the verb or the noun 'produce', but it would then be important to differentiate 'product', 'production' and 'productivity', which could become $prod^t$, $prod^n$ and $prod^y$.

Suffixes may also be attached to symbols. If one has chosen ∞ to represent 'international', then 'internationalization' could be simply ∞n.

Parentheses

Sometimes an interpreter is aware of what the speaker has said and has fully registered it intellectually but does not have the time to note it down. If they are sure they can remember the detail of the point made by the speaker but are worried that they might forget to make the point at all in their interpretation if they do not note it, they can indicate the existence of the point by including a parenthesis in their notes. This parenthesis is there merely as a warning sign to the interpreter, saying, 'Be careful! There is that other point you must include here'. This sign is particularly useful if a speaker makes a digression that is otherwise difficult to fit logically into your notes, or if they tell a colourful anecdote or a joke which, precisely because it is a vivid passage, is easy to re-narrate, provided one remembers to include it. In the case of an anecdote or joke the interpreter can also choose to note the parenthesis, and within it to write one key word which should trigger off memory of the story, or even write the word *joke*, just to remind themselves to tell the joke at that juncture.

Numbering

It almost goes without saying that interpreters can often make life easier for themselves by numbering points in their notes, just as we mentioned above that they might find it useful to number points in their mind to enhance their analysis of structure and their recall of a speech. If a speaker numbers in their actual speech, then you should definitely follow their numbering. But even if a speaker does not number, it may help to introduce your own numbering in notes, provided of course their structure is sufficiently clear to make numbering possible.

   In such numbering, whether it comes directly from the speaker or whether it is the interpreter's initiative, there may be not just points but also sub-points, and even sub-sub-points. In such cases the interpreter must take care to have a watertight numbering system. If the main points are numbered with Arabic numerals, then sub-points must be noted with something else, letters or Roman numerals, for example. Otherwise the notes and the subsequent interpretation run the risk of being extremely confused and confusing.

Efficiency

In all use of abbreviations and symbols, interpreters must seek out the most efficient form of notes. This means they must draw upon the widest possible range of signs. They should use mathematical signs such as +, $-$, =, <, >, £, ±, and so on. They should also call upon punctuation marks: for example *!* can be used to mean 'important', just as) and *?* can be used to mean 'supply' and 'demand'. Arrows of all possible forms and directions can be used, as described above. Letters of different scripts can be used. Interpreters who can read music can borrow from musical notation. Those who are more visually inclined can even use schematic drawings: a simple ladder plus the suffix *-n* could express 'escalation' in a military conflict. Reminiscences from school or university days can help, with the table of elements being used from chemistry and the Newtonian abbreviations from the laws of motion learnt in physics classes. The list is endless.

The variety of potential sources of symbols and abbreviations, plus the requirement that notes should always be logically meaningful to their user, means that interpreters should let their imagination play in devising notes. It is spontaneously, instinctively, through letting their mind wander and using lateral thinking, association of ideas, that each interpreter will come up with the system of symbols and abbreviations best suited to them.

At the same time, the search for efficiency means there are two things the interpreter should *not* do. First, they should not develop symbols and abbreviations that are so complicated that they actually take longer to note down than writing notes long-hand, or than using ad hoc, but perfectly obvious, abbreviations. If one has a well-developed system of symbols and abbreviations, particularly if the system admits combinations of different symbols and abbreviations, it is easy to fall into the trap of taking notes which are more trouble than they are worth.

Second, there are many things that interpreters should not write down in their notes. The verb 'to be' can usually be omitted, being understood in context by default. 'The Secretary-General is pleased that...' can be noted *Sec-Gen pleased...*, The only thing that needs to be noted is the tense or mode, reading the present tense by default. So 'the Secretary-General would be pleased if...' can be noted *Sec-Gen plêased...*. The word *not*, and the idea of negation in general, need not be written long-hand in notes but can be expressed by crossing out the notion to be negated. Then there are so many words that do not need to be noted, either because they will re-emerge automatically in the interpretation from context, or because they are words which have little intrinsic meaning but exist to oil the syntax, so to speak, of a language. An example of the former would be: *The working party has submitted its report to the steering group.* In context it may be obvious that the only operative verb could be *to submit*, in which case this could be noted:

The examples of the latter are legion. Words such as *get*, *make* and *do* can almost always be omitted from notes. The word *that*, used in reported speech or in conjunctional phrases, is unnecessary in notes. Relative pronouns can very often be omitted. And so on. Each interpreter should work on honing down their notes and eliminating all the possible dross.

The Language in which to Note

Student interpreters invariably ask whether they should take notes in the source or the target language. There are arguments in favour of both.

The advantage of noting in the source language is that you will not be held up or bothered by questions of translation while taking the notes. You have a better guarantee of having a full set of notes at the end of a speech. The interpreter can rely on their interpreting ability, and in particular mastery of their mother tongue, to provide the right rendering in the target language on the basis of notes in the source language. Further, notes in the source language have the particular superiority that if a speaker uses a word or concept very specific to the culture of the source language, and which can only be expressed by a circumlocution or through an explanation in the target language, then noting in the source language will be much more efficient and will probably provide for a better quality oral rendering.

However, there are also advantages in noting in the target language. Above all, if you note in the source language the temptation of noting words, not ideas, is much greater. You can be intellectually lazy and just follow the speaker passively, noting their words. Then, when it comes to interpreting the speech, you find that you have not really assimilated the ideas and are not in a position to reconstruct the speech. If, on the other hand, you force yourself to note in the target language, then you are obliged to use the mental processes that should be at play in interpreting. You are genuinely processing the information while listening to it. That is why we give a slight preference to noting in the target language.

That said, the important thing is that the question as to which language to note in is really pretty irrelevant: if the question is asked it should be answered in a pragmatic, non-dogmatic way. There are several reasons for this. First, a large share of notes will be in a symbolic or abbreviated form, and as such in a kind of metalanguage which is neither the source nor the target language.

Second, language is composed not just of words but also of grammar and syntax. It may well be that some words are noted in a way that is recognizably part of either the source language or the target language. But the overall form of the notes will be cryptic, and those words will not necessarily be related to other words in the notes in a way that respects the grammar or syntax of either of the two languages in question.

Third, there is no reason why notes have to be dogmatically in the one or the other language. The two can be combined at will. Indeed, interpreters may choose to note things in any way they want, just for reasons of convenience, and may even wish to use words from a third language, perhaps because those words are very short and easy to note in that language, or because the interpreter has lived for a long time in the culture of that third language and the notes just come naturally to them in it. Thus, for example, an interpreter interpreting from German into French may choose to note some words in, say, Italian.

The conclusion, then, is that interpreters should not worry so much about the question of source or target language for notes. It is advisable to choose the one or the other as a rule, for clarity's sake, otherwise the interpreter may be very confused by their own notes. But thereafter flexibility is of the order of the day. As mentioned above, we give a slight preference to the target language. But if a speaker expresses a notion that is very specific to their culture and thus difficult to note in the target language, or if an interpreter simply has a momentary blank and cannot remember how to say a word in the target language, then they should avoid wasting time and just note it in the source language.

The interpreter's notes will mostly not be 'in' this or that language. They will contain symbols and abbreviations, words from two or even more languages, and will be in a cryptic form – the diagonal layout with a left-hand margin reserved for specific purposes – which does not refer to the grammar and syntax of any particular language.

When to Note

When deciding when to note, the interpreter is faced with a dilemma. On the one hand, they wish to start noting as quickly as possible, to avoid being left behind by the speaker. On the other, it is axiomatic that one can only note what one has understood, and the interpreter is aware that they should be working with ideas, not words in isolation. The logical consequence of this second point is that the interpreter should wait until they have understood a complete idea before noting it, which runs counter to the need to be as close as possible to the speaker.

This question is similar to the one facing a simultaneous interpreter who wishes to know when they should start speaking in simultaneous. They don't want to be left behind by the speaker but they wish to work with ideas they have understood in order to talk coherently and meaningfully in the booth. The answer, however, is not the same for the consecutive and the simultaneous interpreter.

First, the consecutive interpreter is more limited in their note-taking by the speed they can write than is the simultaneous interpreter by the speed of their delivery in the booth. The simultaneous interpreter can always accelerate to catch up with a speaker, even if it means speaking unnaturally fast for a few moments; the consecutive interpreter taking notes is under more time pressure and is rarely in a position to accelerate at will.

Second, when the simultaneous interpreter is making a choice about their final delivery, their decision will determine directly what their delegates hear; the consecutive interpreter is taking a decision about notes, which, we repeat, are only an aid to the interpreter, relieving the interpreter's memory and helping them find the structure of a speech more easily. The notes being a means to an end, they do not have to be noted in a correct grammatical and syntactical way.

Thus the risk of being left behind is greater for the consecutive interpreter than for the simultaneous, and the consecutive interpreter has the freedom to note words and expressions in an order in which they would not say them. For these two reasons we would argue that for the consecutive interpreter the priority is to start taking notes as quickly as possible. For a given speech, they could, and should, start taking notes earlier than a simultaneous interpreter would start speaking (the question of timing in simultaneous will be dealt with at greater length in the next chapter).

Noting as quickly as possible does not mean that one should note every notion as soon as it is said. If a speaker begins with a noun or a nominal group, such as *the royal family*, the interpreter cannot know how that will fit in, in the subsequent sentence, and should therefore not note it. *The royal family* may be the active subject of the sentence, but it may also be followed by a passive form, as in *The royal family has been attacked by the tabloid press*. In this example it is all the more important to avoid noting *the royal family* immediately in the 'subject' position if the passive form is to all intents and purposes not used in the target language, which means that the interpreter has no convenient means of switching the sentence round to make *the tabloid press* the subject.

However, the consecutive interpreter can still begin noting very quickly in this sentence. As soon as they hear *has been attacked* they know how, grammatically, *the royal family* fits in. If the interpreter wishes to keep the passive form in their rendering they can begin their notes with *the royal family* in the subject position, provided they have some clear way of indicating the passive. Their notes could then read:

> royal family
>> attacked __|
>>> tabloid press

We repeat, the interpreter must know from this that the form is passive – for example by decreeing that *attacked* is necessarily a passive form – otherwise the notes could mislead them into thinking that the royal family has attacked the press, which is far from impossible.

On the other hand, the interpreter may choose to note the sentence in the active form. The answer then is to note *royal family* immediately, but to put it in the position for the object of the sentence. Then you note *has attacked* in the verb position, and lastly the subject in the appropriate place. This enables the interpreter to note in a way conducive to a good oral rendering while preventing them from lagging behind the speaker. This technique works well also if other circumstantial elements are added to the sentence. For example, if the sentence were *The royal family has been attacked in the most savage way over the last five years by the tabloid press,* the interpreter can still note first *the royal family* in the object position and then add the other elements progressively. This means the notes, before *by the tabloid press* has been said, would look as follows:

> attack | 5y
>   royal family

and as the speaker reaches the end of their sentence the interpreter merely has to fill in the subject in the notes.

Another difference between the timing of note-taking in consecutive and speaking in simultaneous concerns sentences beginning with subordinate or relative clauses in the original. As will be seen in the next chapter, it is better to avoid beginning sentences in simultaneous with a relative such as *Because of the structural overcapacity in the steel sector....* On the contrary, in consecutive it is important to note this clause immediately, particularly the link-word *because.* The speaker may go off at a tangent and never provide a main clause to the sentence. This is embarrassing in simultaneous if one has been following the speaker too closely, but it does not matter in consecutive. The interpreter will register this mentally and adjust their notes accordingly, or may even be able to adjust their interpretation without bothering about changing their notes. At all times, the consecutive interpreter is in the happy position of not being bound by their notes. A speaker may argue, 'Because proposition A, proposition B'. The interpreter may note that with exactly the same structure, but when it comes to interpreting that passage, for stylistic reasons, or reasons of clarity or whatever, they may present it as 'Proposition A, therefore proposition B'. The interpreter has not presented things in exactly the same way as the speaker, and, of more interest to us here, has not even presented things as they were noted. But that is irrelevant, as long as the meaning conveyed is the same as that of the speaker.

Lastly on the question of when to note, we should recall what we have already said about numbers and lists. When an interpreter senses that these are coming, they should metaphorically drop everything else and be right behind the speaker to note them immediately.

In conclusion, the interpreter should note as soon as possible. They do not have to wait for a complete sentence or even a complete grammatical clause to start noting. Nonetheless, they should note only insofar as they can see where an element fits into its context. They should not feel obliged to note things in the order in which they will be read back, but can begin with any out of subject, verb or object, or any link or circumstantial element.

How to Read Back Notes

It may seem strange even to mention how to read back notes. However, interpreters should be aware of the risk of communicating less well because of looking too much at their notes and not enough at their audience. This risk is particularly great if the interpreter takes fairly complete notes. Interpreters, like any public speaker, must learn the art of glancing down at their notes to remind them of what they are to say next and then delivering that part of the text while looking at the audience. The clearer the notes, both in content and in layout, the easier this will be. And the clearer the ideas in the interpreter's mind, the more cursory can the glances down at the notes be.

There is a specific technique that interpreters can try to develop, and which can be compared to a pianist reading music while playing but not sight-reading. The pianist who has practised a piece is in a similar situation to the consecutive interpreter: essentially they know what they want to play but the sheet music is there to remind them. The pianist looks at the opening bars and then starts playing, and continues reading ahead of the notes they are playing, their eyes on the music always being a little ahead of their fingers on the keyboard. Similarly, the interpreter should look at the first page of their notes then start speaking while looking up at their audience. As the interpreter moves toward the end of the passage they have looked at, they glance down at their notes again to read the next passage. In other words, they do not wait until they have finished one passage to look again at their notes, which would mean that the interpretation would become jerky, reading then speaking, reading then speaking. Rather, the interpreter, while still talking, is already reading ahead, preparing the next passage, thus providing for a smooth, uninterrupted and efficient interpretation.

Exercises

Getting started on note-taking

These exercises are above all to help students begin note-taking without falling into the trap of taking too many notes and concentrating so much on the notes that they fail to continue to apply active analytical listening. In all of the exercises below it is recommended that the students actually do the speech in consecutive and do not limit themselves to listening and note-taking. They must understand that the important thing is the end product (the interpretation) and that the notes are not an end in themselves. Exercises (a), (b) and (c) are recommended in this sequence before letting students loose on a full set of notes. The others may simply be useful if certain students need to concentrate particularly on particular elements in speeches.

(a) Make a fairly easy speech with quite a few numbers and/or dates and tell the students that they may note only the numbers and dates. (Check that they respect this instruction.) A good type of speech to do would be a historical, chronological narration where the students can no doubt remember the sequence of events but need notes for the figures and dates.

(b) Use a similar speech but include a number of proper names and instruct the students that this time they may note only the numbers, dates and proper names.

(c) Use a speech of average difficulty and instruct the students to note only the main ideas.

(d) Use a highly structured, argumentative speech and instruct the students to note only the link words that they would, in a full set of notes, put in the left-hand margin.

(e) The same as (d), but where 'points of view' are to be noted.

(f) A combination of (d) and (e).

4. Simultaneous Interpreting

In one sense simultaneous interpretation is the same thing as consecutive interpretation. They are the same in that both mean listening, understanding, analyzing and re-expressing. In both cases the interpreter is indulging in the same basic intellectual activities. Moreover, in both cases the interpreter is fulfilling the same function as a conduit for communication. It is easy for the interpreter in simultaneous, physically cut-off from the meeting in a sound-proofed booth behind double-glazing, to forget that they are part of the meeting, that they are carrying out this essential communication function. It is important to avoid this trap, to try to sense the atmosphere of a meeting through the panes of glass, watching the body language of delegates and picking up any non-verbal information they can, using the appropriate intonation in their interpretation, rather than slipping into a monotonous drawl. Simultaneous interpreters should maintain eye contact as much as possible with delegates and even use gestures in the booth, even though nobody may be watching those gestures.

This, incidentally, is why proper design of conference rooms involving interpreting is of such importance and why proper visibility must be guaranteed for interpreters. Meeting organizers who feel they can put interpreters in booths with inadequate vision of the meeting room or even 'blind booths' have a recipe for poor interpretation. This is also a consideration to be borne in mind when envisaging video-conferences involving interpreting. It is too early to make any pronouncements on the feasibility or desirability of video-conferences where interpreters would not be in the same place as their delegates and would be watching them on television monitors. But there is at the least a risk of interpreters feeling alienated from the meeting in such circumstances and finding it difficult or impossible to provide high quality interpretation. As video-conferencing becomes ever more frequent both interpreters and meeting organizers should give the matter very serious thought.

Thus, to resume our argument, we stress the unchanged nature of the basic interpreting function and the intellectual processes involved. Much of what has already been said about consecutive therefore also applies to simultaneous.

At the same time it is obvious that simultaneous and consecutive are quite different. Essentially, there are two fundamental differences, which create two added difficulties in simultaneous, an acoustic one and an intellectual one.

The acoustic difficulty is that in consecutive the interpreter listens first, then speaks. In simultaneous, the interpreter has to speak and listen at the same time, which is an unnatural activity and has to be cultivated.

The intellectual difficulty is that in consecutive, when the interpreter opens their mouth they have heard the whole speech and should know where they are going. Sometimes points that were unclear or even words that were unknown at the moment at which they were pronounced by the speaker become clear to the interpreter in the overall context of the speech. The interpreter has no such luxury in simultaneous. You do not know where the speaker is going, even as you speak. And this is true both at the macro level of the speech and at the micro level. That is, at macro level you do not know where the speech as a whole is headed; at micro level, you do not know how an individual sentence will continue, perhaps even something as basic as whether it will be in the positive or the negative form.

Assuming one can cope in consecutive with the basic elements of interpreting – listening, understanding, analyzing and re-expressing – techniques have to be developed in simultaneous to cope with these two types of difficulty.

The Acoustic Difficulties of Simultaneous Interpreting

Use of equipment

First, you should stack all the cards in your favour by making the best possible use of the equipment available. Despite various possible refinements a simultaneous interpreter's equipment is basically a set of headphones and a microphone. To deal with the headphones first, interpreters need to be able to hear both the speaker and themselves. One should not think that the speaking side of simultaneous interpreting takes place automatically and that you do not need to monitor yourself, or even that the interpreter will necessarily hear their own voice in their head. Therefore, the interpreter must wear the headphones in such a way as to be able to hear the speaker clearly but also hear their own output and monitor it all the time. To do this there are essentially two options. The first is for the interpreter to wear both ear-pieces of a pair of headphones half on and half off each ear, slightly to the front of the ear. This enables one to hear the speaker clearly, the sound coming through the headphones quite satisfactorily into the interpreter's ears while leaving the ears sufficiently uncovered for you to hear your own voice. The second option is simply to wear one earphone fully on one ear and to leave the other ear totally uncovered. This leaves each ear to perform a different task. Neurolinguistic research over the last decade has tended to show that, because of the cerebral lateralization of language functions, there may be an advantage in privileging one ear for the earphone. For a *right*-handed interpreter, there appears to be an advantage in covering the *left* ear with the earphone, using that ear to listen to the source language. The right ear is left free to listen to the interpreter's own output in the target language. This rule applies both when you are working into your mother tongue and out of it into a retour language. Readers interested in pursuing this question can refer in particular to Lambert (1990) and more generally to the work of Fabbro and Gran (see Further Reading at the end of this book). Without in any way calling into question the value and interest of this research, we should nevertheless encourage students and young interpreters to try out different positions to see which one suits them best.

The interpreter controls the volume at which they listen to the original. It is important to keep this volume as low as feasibly possible. Both the original and the interpreter's own voice have to be listened to, but they should not become like rivals trying to outshout one another. If you put up the volume high, then in order to listen to yourself you have to raise your voice; but this drowns out the original, so you put up the volume even higher; and you end up in a vicious circle. This is very bad for your hearing in the long run. Straining your voice for three or more hours a day can only be bad. It is unpleasant for delegates to have an interpreter shouting at them for hours on end. And it is unbearable for the other interpreters who are working in the same booth. Therefore, the interpreter should have the volume low, at a comfortable hearing level *if they are not speaking*. Then, if you interpret in a normal conversational voice you should be able to hear both the original and yourself adequately.

As to the microphone, for the comfort of the delegates listening to the interpreter you must try to make sure that the sound output level is as regular as possible. The level of the interpreter's voice should remain fairly constant, a normal conversational one as just mentioned, and the interpreter should sit directly in front of the microphone at a constant distance from it, avoiding major movements either side to side or forwards and backwards. For most equipment currently on the market, speaking at a distance of thirty centimetres from the microphone is about right.

There are occasions, as mentioned in chapter one, when simultaneous is 'chuchotage', done without technical equipment. In such circumstances the interpreter must similarly ensure the working conditions are optimal. This means sitting (or standing) where you are sure you can hear the speaker, and being in a position to speak sufficiently softly so as not to hinder their listening or upset other participants in the meeting who are listening to the original. As a general rule this means you are entitled to disregard protocol and may even ask to change places with a delegate.

In no circumstances should interpreters attempt to interpret what they have not heard. If the working conditions are so bad that they absolutely cannot perform their function correctly they should inform the meeting organizers and either cease work, offer consecutive interpreting as an alternative, or wait for the necessary arrangements to be made.

Cultivating Split Attention

In normal circumstances people concentrate on one thing at a time, and in speech in particular they listen to one line of discourse at a time. The interpreter has to listen to two lines of discourse. How does one deal with this?

First, one has to recognize the need to listen consciously to oneself when interpreting. This is another difference from 'normal' speech where one talks automatically: you know what you want to say, the words come tumbling out of their own accord, and you do not need to pay attention to grammar, pronunciation, etc. But for the interpreter, working under stress, anything can happen. If the interpreter is not monitoring their own output they can be ungrammatical, pronounce words incorrectly, forget words, such that they may even flatly contradict themselves in two successive sentences by forgetting to say the word *not* in one of them. Thus, you have to be aware of the need to monitor yourself and to make a conscious effort to do so. Just as the consecutive interpreter has learned to listen in a different, active, analytical way, now the simultaneous interpreter, while not ceasing to listen actively to the speaker, must learn to listen carefully and critically to themselves.

Second, you have to accept that if you try to concentrate on more than one thing at a time you increase the risk of error in at least one of those areas. To minimize the chances of error when listening to two related but distinct discourses, the interpreter's total level of concentration must be kept at its maximum. The interpreter must be focused totally on what the speaker and they themselves are saying, and cannot let their mind stray to extraneous matters such as the speaker's accent, linguistic or other idiosyncrasies, still less to visual details in the room, the weather outside or any other thing unrelated to the meeting.

But we can go further than merely telling you to concentrate as hard as you can. The simultaneous interpreter's concentration can be disturbed more insidiously than in the ways just mentioned. The interpreter may come across a word in the original they do not know at all, or perhaps a word they do know but are not sure how best to render in the target language. If a word is not known, except in the very rare cases where such ignorance makes it impossible to render an idea correctly, the interpreter must ignore the word in question and get on with the job of interpreting the sense of the speaker's sentence. If a word or expression is known but the interpreter has a number of options as to how to render it, they must make a split-second decision and go clearly for one option, even if in retrospect that is not the option the interpreter would have preferred. For example, a delegate may say, *To make such a fine distinction is to use a captious argument.* Now, *captious* is hardly a word that one uses every day and that will necessarily spring to mind. All kinds of things could shoot through the interpreter's mind: sophistry, quibbling, splitting hairs, and so on. The interpreter is well-advised, in context, assuming the speaker is responding to another delegate, to say, *That's just splitting hairs*, even if they may afterwards feel this is the wrong linguistic register, and even if it does not do full justice to the two notions of 'fine distinction' and 'captious argument'. That is better than trying to render every word and ending up saying, *Such a fine distinction, splitting hairs like that, is really... um... this is really sophistry, your argument is a... fallacy, that is, I feel this is captious reasoning.* Victory! The interpreter has found the 'right word'! Not at all. The interpreter, by proceeding in this way, has wasted a lot of time and energy, may have missed another important idea in the original, and will probably have irritated the delegates with all this prevarication.

This should not be understood as pleading in favour of sloppy, approximate interpreting, saying the first vaguely appropriate thing that springs to mind. The interpreter must get it right, but they must get it right first time round. Hedging round ideas and piling up synonyms is usually counterproductive. Whether in the case of unknown words or in the case of words where the interpreter is spoiled for choice, *the simultaneous interpreter must not get 'hung up' on the words.*

Another distraction for the interpreter comes from the feeling or maybe even the knowledge that they have missed something out or interpreted a passage less well than they might have. There is no point thinking back over what has already happened and worrying about it. That will only reduce the interpreter's level of concentration on the job in hand. It is rather like a chess player who missed an opportunity to capture the opponent's queen and realizes only afterwards. If they continue to worry about it there is every chance they will lose; if they concentrate on the present situation on the chessboard they still have every chance of winning.

To sum up, cultivating split attention is an unnatural activity. Significantly, it is often the element of conference interpreting which most mystifies non-interpreters. The way to cope with it is to maintain a maximum level of concentration and very deliberately and consciously address your attention to the two discourses in question. In one way simultaneous can be compared to playing the piano, which is also an unnatural form of behaviour. The pianist has to learn the right hand, then the left, then learns to coordinate both, in much the same way as the interpreter learns to listen to two speeches at the same time.

Listening to Oneself in Simultaneous Interpreting

The critical listening to oneself mentioned above concerns both content and form. In terms of content you must be constantly checking that the interpretation is a correct and, insofar as is necessary, a complete rendering of the original. In terms of form you must check that you are being grammatical and making sense (as opposed to talking literally nonsense). Here, again, the battle is half won if you can make life easy for yourself, and that can be done by applying just a few basic rules.

The first rule is to speak, as far as is possible, in short, simple sentences. This approach is to be adopted however long and complex the sentences of the speaker may be. It is obvious that if you launch into long, complicated sentences with subordinate and relative clauses, the risk of losing the thread of your own sentence, and therefore making a mistake or forgetting what you want to say, is much greater. Conversely, with a simple sentence structure it is much easier to check up on yourself, and if ever you do make a slip of the tongue to correct it quickly and easily.

When we say 'short, simple sentences', we mean sentences composed of only one principal clause. This may seem a rather extreme approach to take, and some interpreters might be worried that their work may end up sounding too childish. We feel, however, that it is difficult to go too far in expressing yourself in simple sentences, and that this has the dual advantage of making it easier for the interpreter to listen critically to their own output and providing ease of listening for the delegates. Delegates are usually delighted to have everything chopped up into small, pre-digested units for them, provided the ideas are expressed clearly.

Second, you should make sure, in listening to yourself, that each individual sentence has sense, grammatically and logically. If you can force yourself into the habit of *never* saying anything that is nonsense or meaningless, then you have automatically eliminated a large number of potential sources of error. Moreover, once the interpreter has made sure they are making sense at the level of each sentence, then it is that much easier to monitor the overall coherence and logic of their own interpretation.

Third, although one might argue that this is just a specific case of the previous rule, the interpreter must always finish their sentences. An unfinished sentence means by definition that the interpreter has stopped making sense. The most annoying and unsettling thing for a delegate is to be left hanging in the air by their interpreter because of a sentence such as: *The increase in sales tax on these products over the last five years has meant that [silence]*. Delegates may fail to notice omissions and errors, and even if they do notice them they may forgive the interpreter, but knowing that the interpreter can just give up on them like that undermines their confidence in the interpreter totally.

These three points have been presented as an aid to the interpreter in that they facilitate the task of critical listening to oneself in simultaneous. However, they are clearly also important for dealing with what we called the intellectual difficulties of simultaneous, and will be taken up in more detail below.

The 'Golden Rules' of Simultaneous Interpreting

Before moving on to more detailed questions of simultaneous interpreting technique it is useful to take stock at this stage on a number of very basic ideas presented so far. Some might feel it pretentious to present these as 'golden rules', but if all of them are followed, the interpreter will be in a much better position to apply the techniques we are about to discuss.

The simultaneous interpreter must :

- remember they are communicating;
- make the best possible use of the technical facilities;
- ensure they can hear both the speaker and themself clearly;
- never attempt to interpret something they have not heard or acoustically understood;
- maximize concentration;
- not be distracted by focussing attention on individual problematic words;
- cultivate split attention, with active, analytical listening to the speaker and critical monitoring of their own output;
- use, where possible, short, simple sentences;
- be grammatical;
- make sense in every single sentence;
- always finish their sentences.

The Technique of Simultaneous Interpreting

When to Start Speaking?

The first question that arises for an interpreter in simultaneous, 'first' in a literal, chronological sense, is when to start speaking, and thereafter what distance to keep from the speaker. On the one hand it is necessary to give the speaker a certain headstart, because otherwise the interpreter will not have sufficient material to work with in order to say something meaningful; on the other hand the interpreter cannot afford to be too far behind, otherwise they spend the entire speech trying to catch up with the speaker and run the risk of missing out important things.

The first part of the answer to this all-important question has little to do with interpreting technique and is rather more a point of practical psychology. The interpreter should say *something* almost immediately, in order to reassure the participants listening to them. If a speaker begins and the interpreter says absolutely nothing, be it only for a few seconds, because they are waiting for the right moment to begin their interpretation, the participants listening to the interpreter may become very nervous, turn round and make signs at the interpreters' booth, or even interrupt proceedings to complain there is no interpretation. The interpreter must therefore make at least some sound. One of the safest things one can say is *Thank you, chairman*, (or, if one is interpreting the chairperson, to say simply 'thank you' to the previous speaker), even if the speaker has not taken the trouble to be so polite.

Having dealt with this minor point of psychology, however, the interpreter is still faced with the difficult question of when to start interpreting what the speaker is actually saying. It is important to recognize that the answer to the question cannot be given in terms of time: 'Stay x seconds behind the speaker' (we could add that, even if we wished to pin things down in terms of seconds, everything moves so fast in simultaneous that the time-lag would sometimes be less than a second and would practically never exceed a few seconds: five seconds is an eternity in simultaneous). Rather, the answer depends on the grammar and syntax used by the speaker, the speed of the speaker, and the source and target languages. This means the answer will vary for practically every speech: there is no single rule for when one begins speaking.

However, we must try and give some guidance on this question, and the best way to begin is to be pragmatic and go back to first principles. The first basic principle is that the interpreter should try to begin speaking 'as soon as possible' (a notion that we shall qualify). The interpreter cannot wait for the speaker to finish one sentence before they say something, doing a kind of mini-consecutive of that sentence while waiting for the next one. The chances are that the interpreter will end up rendering only one sentence out of two. Because they think in terms of sentences, their attention will be focused on, say, the first sentence, listening first, then speaking, but while they are saying the first sentence the speaker has moved on to the second one, which the interpreter – still focusing on the first sentence – will have difficulty concentrating on. The interpreter will then pick up the third sentence but may miss the fourth, and so on. Second, the interpreter who works in this way will have a tendency to rush through the sentence when they are speaking, blurting things out to the detriment of clarity and elegance, precisely because they are in a hurry to stop speaking to try and listen to the next sentence. Third, the sentence is a completely arbitrary and unmanageable unit to work with: *I agree* is a sentence. At the other extreme there are delegates whose sentences have the length and complexity of those in Kafka or Proust, sentences that it is impossible to use as units in a simultaneous.

We must thus reject simultaneous being done as a kind of sequence of accelerated mini-consecutives. However, having said the interpreter must begin speaking 'as soon as possible', what is it that makes it possible for the interpreter to speak? Here we find our second basic principle: the interpreter must be able to express something meaningful if they are to open their mouth. This means in turn that they must have understood in the source language some meaningful notion that they can put into the target language. The speaker must have enunciated some 'slice' or 'chunk' of speech that forms a meaningful whole and which the interpreter can therefore use as raw material for their own output.

This notion of a meaningful section of speech brings us on to the notion of a 'unit of meaning'. The unit of meaning is a notion identified and developed by Marianne Lederer and Danica Seleskovitch, two eminent teachers of interpreting and researchers in translation studies, in the framework of their activities at the École Supérieure d'Interprètes et de Traducteurs in Paris. The notion is used to provide a descriptive model of the way a simultaneous interpreter proceeds.

We understand a unit of meaning to be a cognitive representation in the mind of the listener (for our purposes the interpreter) of the intended meaning of the speaker. This cognitive representation is formed from the words just spoken by the speaker and the application to those words of other cognitive information available to the interpreter. The other cognitive information may come from the interpreter's background knowledge; it may come from the general context of a meeting (a speaker refers to comments made by other participants or to a document used in the meeting, etc.); or it may come from the immediate context of the speech, such as the previous sentence or other parts of the same sentence. The cognitive representation in the mind of the listener is therefore not the same thing as the words spoken by the speaker: it is a product of them and other elements available to the interpreter.

What is the link between a unit of meaning, as a notion, and the decision as to when to start a simultaneous? The unit of meaning is a *micro-component* of the meaning of a speech. It is the succession of units of meaning, relating to one another and merging into one another, that forms the overall meaning of a speech. The minimum length of a unit of meaning is determined by the shortest possible passage that may engender a clear cognitive representation in the mind of the listener. This means that a unit of meaning can be one word. *Death, water, France, libraries*, may all generate cognitive representations in the mind of the listener. The maximum length of a unit of meaning is determined by the length of an oral passage that can remain present to the ear at any one given moment. This means that a unit of meaning will be the product of a sequence of words lasting at most a few seconds (seven or eight words, according to Lederer and Seleskovitch), and in any case not more than a sentence. The unit of meaning can therefore be taken as being the smallest usable unit for the interpreter, who may thus begin speaking once a unit of meaning is given.

It is clear from this that a unit of meaning is of variable length and cannot be systematically related to grammatical categories. As mentioned, a unit of meaning may be formed from one word. Take the sentence: *Britain, despite the ruling of the Court of Human Rights in Strasbourg, has decided to maintain its position on the treatment of prison inmates*. Here the word *Britain* may generate a clear cognitive representation in the mind of the interpreter, particularly if in context they are aware that it means the British government, and the interpreter might choose to start interpreting (although the risk of starting so soon will be seen shortly below). A unit of meaning may come from just a little more than one word. For example: *The Minister of the Interior does not intend to propose any change to the rules governing treatment of prison inmates*. Here, the first unit of meaning will probably be *the Minister of the Interior*.

But these are nice easy sentences that begin with the grammatical subject.

The first unit of meaning may be significantly longer. For example, if we rearrange our first example we could have: *Despite the ruling of the Court of Human Rights in Strasbourg, the British prison authorities have decided to maintain their position on the treatment of inmates*. The interpreter has to wait at least until *Human Rights* to have a unit of meaning; they can hardly be expected to say anything before then. Further on, we no longer have *Britain*, but *the British prison authorities*, which has to be taken as a unit of meaning.

The length of a unit of meaning has so far been seen to vary depending essentially on linguistic considerations such as syntax. But the variation in length may also come from the other cognitive information available to the interpreter. Let's assume the speaker says exactly the same thing as in the previous example – *Despite the ruling...* – but that the ruling in question has been the object of discussion for the last half hour. The interpreter will not need the extra information supplied by the speaker to know which ruling is meant, and can form a unit of meaning just from the words *Despite the ruling*.

One could therefore try to establish a basic rule on the timing of simultaneous work: begin speaking when you have understood a unit of meaning, and remain one unit behind the speaker, proceeding from unit to unit. The great advantage of this approach is that in this way you should never be too far behind the speaker, will always have something meaningful to say, and, because of the flexibility of the notion of unit of meaning, will be able to structure your own interpretation in a flexible way, making yourself more master of the situation.

However, despite the undoubted value of the concept of unit of meaning, there is another way of setting about the question as to when to start interpreting in simultaneous and how far to remain behind the speaker. Such an alternative method is necessary in that it is more practical, and there are circumstances when working with units of meaning is insufficient.

First, the notion of a unit of meaning is not a very handy one for an interpreter to use consciously in the heat of the action of a simultaneous interpretation. And to be fair to Lederer and Seleskovitch, as mentioned above, the origin and prime use of the concept lie in the ex-post analysis of how interpreters work and more generally of how people understand discourse, rather than in a pedagogical context; its value is essentially descriptive, not prescriptive.

Second, when interpreting from certain source languages, working systematically from units of meaning may mean waiting an awful long time. For example, a speaker of a Germanic language may begin a sentence with:

> On the by the Canadian delegation proposed and by the American delegation supported highly important, fully understandable, but perhaps, in the current by considerable monetary turbulence marked circumstances, a little premature textual amendments...

(In real English this is: 'On the textual amendments proposed by the Canadian delegation and supported by the American delegation, which are highly important, fully understandable, but perhaps a little premature in these times of considerable monetary instability...'.)

With a sentence like this, which we admit is problematic whatever method an interpreter adopts, more analysis than the identification of the first unit of meaning is necessary if the interpreter does not want to wait until 'textual amendments'.

Third, working from units of meaning may also force the interpreter to make long, artificial pauses in the middle of sentences, rather than deliberately making the pauses between sentences, which would increase the ease of listening for delegates. For example, there may be a clear unit of meaning provided at the beginning of a sentence, followed by a lengthy digression such that it is difficult to say anything at all:

> Britain, following the ruling of the Court of Human Rights in Strasbourg, which I am sure you are all aware of, at least in the broad outline if not in all of its details, seeing as it has had a lot of publicity in the European press, has decided...

It is of course possible to interpret this in simultaneous by proceeding from one unit of meaning to another. But if the interpreter begins in a split second by saying *Britain*, they may find themselves waiting unnaturally long for the next unit of meaning which links up with the subject before they say something else.

For all these reasons, I feel an alternative method has to be sought. It must be stressed, however, that this does not call into question the validity of the unit of meaning analysis of how interpreters work. A good interpreter *does* proceed by operating with units of meaning. But they may do so quite unconsciously, and in order to take conscious decisions about what to say when, which an interpreter does practically every second of their professional life, a more pragmatic approach is needed. This approach, I would argue, should be less abstract and intellectual, and more linguistic.

To provide an alternative, practical rule as to when to start speaking in simultaneous, again we must return to first principles. As in the discussion of units of meaning we can assume that the interpreter must start speaking as soon as possible, and that "as soon as possible" means that they must have understood something meaningful in order to have something meaningful to say. However, we can now add the basic principle that the interpreter must always speak coherently and grammatically, and in particular that they must always finish their sentences. With all this in mind, we can now say that the interpreter can start speaking *once they have enough material from the speaker to finish their own (interpreted) sentence*. The interpreter may of course begin a sentence with one idea in mind as to how to finish it and then choose to change tack, but as long as they are coherent and faithful to the speaker that is not a problem in itself.

This approach has a number of advantages. First, provided the interpreter does not launch into a sentence without having at least one way of finishing it, they should never commit the cardinal sin of leaving a sentence unfinished. This will remain true even when the speaker is a poor orator who uses long, complicated sentences which they themselves are ultimately incapable of finishing. The interpreter will express those ideas that have been grammatically formulated by the speaker, and can just drop odd ends of sentences or clauses that are never completed, for example subjects without verbs, or transitive verbs without an object.

Second, if the interpreter is sure of being able to finish a sentence when they start saying something, this makes it much easier for them to pause between sentences rather than in the middle of sentences as they seek a way of expressing themselves. This will make their delivery that much more natural and easier to follow.

Third, if the end of a sentence is 'in sight' as soon as it begins, this will help the interpreter to think and speak in short, simple sentences, the desirability of which has already been mentioned.

The way to use this approach can best be explained by using a number of examples, which for convenience will be variations on those already provided in this section.

A clear case where the interpreter is sure to be able to finish their sentence is when the speaker provides a subject, a verb and a direct object, such as:

> Britain has decided to maintain its position on the treatment of prison inmates, despite the ruling of the Court of Human Rights in Strasbourg.

Once the speaker has said *its position*, the interpreter may start. Even if the speaker were to break off into a digression after that, the interpreter is safe. Let's now assume the text is:

> Britain has decided to maintain its position – and I know that this is not totally uncontroversial, following the debate in the working parties and in the plenary session – on the treatment...

Here the interpreter can simply say, 'Britain has decided to maintain its position'. Then they deal with the digression as a different sentence, or even a number of sentences. Last, they return to the main clause of the sentence, perhaps with a reminder of how it fits in with the speaker's argument, using something like 'This position concerns the treatment...'

Of course, the moment at which the interpreter starts speaking will also depend on the speed of the speaker. If the above speaker starts like a racehorse, the interpreter should certainly get going as soon as they hear *position*. If the pace is much slower, an interpreter, particularly an experienced one, may choose to wait for a few more words.

Let's now go back to the original form of the quotation in question, used when discussing units of meaning:

> Britain, despite the ruling of the Court of Human Rights in Strasbourg,
> has decided to maintain its position on the treatment of prison inmates.

This shows clearly that it is dangerous for the interpreter to leap in with *Britain* as soon as they hear it. By saying *Britain* and then having to work out how to deal with the incidental clause ('despite the ruling...'), the interpreter may be forced into a long, unnatural pause in the middle of the sentence. Worse, the incidental clause may become long and unwieldy, and it may be difficult for both the interpreter and the delegates listening to them to link *Britain* up with the relevant verb. In a worst-case scenario the speaker may actually forget that they started with *Britain*, not finishing the sentence at all and leaving the interpreter hanging in the air.

The way for the interpreter to deal with this is to apply the rule of waiting until they have enough material to complete a sentence. This moment, I would contend, is after *Human Rights*. The interpreter begins with the idea of saying, 'The Court of Human Rights has made a ruling'. By the time they have said *Human Rights* the speaker will already have added *in Strasbourg*, which information can then be included by the interpreter. The speaker in the meantime continues with *has decided to maintain...*, enabling the interpreter to deal with the main clause, the subject of which is *Britain*. The final output of the interpreter can now be smoothly delivered as:

> The Court of Human Rights in Strasbourg has made a ruling. Despite
> this, Britain has decided to maintain its position on the treatment of prison
> inmates.

We should note, though, that there may be good grammatical reasons for not starting a sentence as soon as you hear what appear to be the subject. This tends to depend on the source language. If English or a Romance language is being spoken, then a sentence beginning with, say, 'The necessary information' will have *information* as the subject. But in other languages, such as German and Slavic languages, the subject-object relationship may be shown more by case endings than by word order, but the case endings may also be ambiguous, with nominative and accusative sometimes taking the same form.

Thus we may have the sentence: 'The necessary information [possible nominative or accusative] receives in any case my ministry regularly'. When we get to the end of the sentence it is obvious that the subject is *my ministry*, not *information*, and if the interpreter begins a sentence with *information* as the subject they may find themselves in an awkward situation. The situation need not be impossible to resolve. If the interpreter is working into English, for this example, they may fall back on a passive form like *This information is received...*, and other target languages may find it even easier to accommodate such structures. However, a preventative strategy – beginning your sentence only when you know the form it should take – will still leave you more in control of the situation. In the long run it will also be less tiring than a corrective strategy, where the interpreter rushes in and then has to adjust their aim, so to speak, as grammatical and semantic surprises appear.

Note that in certain circumstances the first word that sounds like a subject may even turn out to be an indirect object. Thus the interpreter could hear in a given source language: 'Britain, following the ruling of the Court of Human Rights in Strasbourg, must we say that...'. It is only on hearing *must we say* that the interpreter knows that in the speaker's mouth *Britain* actually meant 'to Britain'. Using the approach already described, if the interpreter begins speaking after *Human Rights*, they can say with no error or unnatural pause: 'The Court of Human Rights in Strasbourg has made its ruling. Following this we must say to Britain that...'.

This approach basically means waiting until there is enough material to finish a sentence and beginning the sentence in such a way as to be sure to finish it. An automatic consequence of this is that the interpreter should avoid beginning their sentences with relative or subordinate clauses. If we return to our basic example, we can produce the following:

> Despite the ruling of the Court of Human Rights in Strasbourg, Britain
> has decided to maintain...

In these circumstances the interpreter definitely has enough material to provide a complete sentence after *Human Rights*, but they should not fall into the trap of beginning their own sentence in the same way as the speaker, namely with *Despite*. Again, if they do follow the speaker too closely the risk is that the speaker's sentence will evolve from this first, subordinate clause in such a way that it is very difficult or even impossible for the interpreter to insert a main clause. The interpreter must, as always, proceed by providing a first, complete sentence: 'The Court of Human Rights in Strasbourg has made a ruling'. Then the notion 'despite' can be brought into the second sentence: 'Despite this, Britain has decided...'.

It is very common for speakers to begin sentences with words or phrases such as *despite, thanks to, given that, on the assumption that, on the under-standing that* or *provided that*. Interpreters should develop a kind of second nature that enables them to avoid following speakers down such roads.

Having now established the conditions under which an interpreter may start speaking in simultaneous, we might ask how they continue: what distance should they keep from the speaker?

Essentially, three things may be said on this point. First, the interpreter should continue as they have begun. The distance from the speaker should remain more or less constant, and in any case the interpreter must always have some way of ending correctly any sentence they begin, not just the first one in a speech.

Second, the interpreter must be flexible. On the one hand, the distance from the speaker should be more or less constant, as we have just said. But on the other, some variation will always be necessary, depending on the speaker's rhythm, style, content, and also depending on specific syntactic difficulties. We shall see later that there are cases, for example when numbers are being quoted, where a different approach has to be adopted to the time-lag between speaker and interpreter.

Third, the interpreter should try to end a speech as close as possible to the speaker. This means that the interpreter, in listening to the speaker, must sense when a speech is drawing to a close. This may be indicated by the content – for example, the speaker arrives at conclusions or summarizes their previous argument – or from the tone of voice. As soon as the interpreter senses the end is in sight they should accelerate their own output a little in order to finish as soon as possible after the speaker. This is very important for an individual interpreter who needs to move on to interpreting the next speaker, who may take the floor very quickly. But it is, if anything, even more important for a pair or trio of interpreters working together in one booth with different passive languages. Let's assume that two interpreters are working together into French from Russian and English, each covering only one language. An English speaker has the floor, comes to the end of their comments, and a Russian delegate, who perhaps is not even listening to interpretation for English, intervenes very quickly. If the interpreter working from English into French takes too long winding up their interpretation, the interpreter working from Russian into French may be seriously handicapped in interpreting the opening remarks of the Russian delegate.

In conclusion on this question, the method chosen for deciding when to begin speaking, and thereafter determining how far one remains behind the speaker, means that the interpreter has to reword the input provided by the speaker. This brings us to the technique discussed in our next point, a technique that lies at the heart of simultaneous interpreting: *reformulation*.

Reformulation

As we have just seen, the need to maintain the right distance from a speaker means that the interpreter has to reformulate the wording of the original. Long, complicated sentences are to be broken down into a series of easier, shorter ones; relative and subordinate clauses can be shifted around within a sentence; active clauses changed into passive or deponent ones (or vice versa); and so on.

This should be seen as an opportunity, not as an unwelcome constraint. The interpreter's job is to convey the speaker's meaning as faithfully as possible. But any translation, written or oral, necessarily changes the form of the original. The most faithful interpretation will merely be the transformation that comes closest to respecting the speaker's intended meaning. And to respect the meaning, one does not necessarily have to copy the exact words of the speaker, nor the order in which the speaker says them. On the contrary, I would defend the paradox that in order to be faithful to the speaker, the interpreter must betray them. The interpreter is rather like a film director adapting a novel for the cinema. The director might want to create an aesthetic effect that is equivalent to the one the novel creates for the reader of the written word. But a film is clearly a different medium. To achieve the desired effect in a different medium the director will have to change many things, thus 'betraying' the novelist. Although the effect sought by the interpreter is not primarily aesthetic, something similar holds for them: the interpreter, rather than attempting to provide a slavish copy of the original, must create in a new medium – the target language – the discourse that will have the same effect on their audience as the speaker's words have on those who understand the source language.

The interpreter must therefore seize upon reformulation as the tool that will enable them to deal with all kinds of difficulties while remaining as true as possible to the speaker. It is difficult to underestimate the importance of this technique, which should really become an inbuilt second nature for the simultaneous interpreter.

A fundamental difficulty that can be dealt with through reformulation is the case where the source language has a word or concept that does not exist in the target language. This problem is not related solely to very specific cultural or institutional notions that are particularly characteristic of a country or a language. Nor do we have to look for complicated philosophical or technical notions to find examples. The simple word 'shallow' does not exist in French in the physical sense of water not being deep, whereas the word 'deep' does. Thus the sentence, 'Barges cannot use the river in summer because it is too shallow', would necessarily have to be reformulated by an interpreter working into French. They could, for example, say, 'Barges cannot use the river in summer because it is not deep enough'.

Such a case is fairly easy to deal with. But there are other cases of words or notions, even very commonly used and fashionable ones, that cannot be directly translated into the target language and which require more judgement on the part of the interpreter. Take the term *cost-effective*. An English-speaking delegate could say, 'We require cost-effective hospital management if our health-care system is to survive'. In some languages there is no direct translation for *cost-effective* but there is for *cost-effectiveness* (or *cost-efficiency*). An interpreter for such a language could try to use the term 'cost-efficiency'. They would then at least have to reformulate the sentence as 'We require [a good level of] cost-efficiency of hospital management if...'. However, the interpreter may also decide that this is a very unnatural, stilted way of expressing things, and look for a different way of conveying the same idea. Alternatively, it may be that not even 'cost-efficiency' exists in the target language and the interpreter is forced into a different form of expression. In both of these latter cases, the interpreter is faced with an unlimited range of possibilities as to how to express the idea. In some languages *cost-effective* may be expressed by the notion 'a good ratio between quality and price'; some may opt for a more casual, less technocratic 'value for money'. In many cases the specific notion 'cost-effective' may disappear as an explicit reference but the idea may be brought out in the sentence as a whole. For example, one might say, 'The [financial] resources of our hospitals must be managed efficiently if...'; or, 'We must make the best possible use of resources in managing our hospitals if...'. And so on. In the last example given, not only has *cost-effective* itself disappeared, but even the components 'cost' and 'efficiency' have as well. And yet the idea expressed is the same.

Sometimes, as we have just seen, words simply do not exist in the target language. On other occasions the words exist but things have to be rephrased because they will sound just too strange if translated literally into the target language. Take the well-known example of the simple sentence, 'He swam across the river' (first used by Vinay and Darbelnet in their *Stylistique comparée* of 1958). The verb 'to swim' exists in French, as does the preposition 'across'. But no French speaker would say 'He swam across the river'. They would say 'He crossed the river by swimming' (*à la nage*). The English preposition is re-expressed via a verb, while the English verb becomes, in French, an adverbial phrase of manner. In such a sentence, for the language pair English-French, reformulation is not merely desirable but is actually necessary. It is not a question of taste, of personal style, as to how one expresses that sentence in French: a literal translation will appear wrong (i.e. bad French) to the listener.

The interpreter, however, should not feel limited to such reformulation only when they feel that not reformulating will produce something in the target language that actually sounds wrong. From our perspective here, the constant objective of the interpreter is to provide a correct translation of the original in a form that sounds as natural and as authentic as possible in the target language: the audience should not feel they are listening to a translation. This means that reformulation should also be used by the interpreter for stylistic reasons. Even though the interpreter is not trying to produce a literary, aesthetically pleasing text for its own sake, they need to make value judgements as to the most appropriate way of saying things in the target language. The fact that such judgements are being made throughout a speech and in real time, in other words continuously and in a pressure situation, illustrates again the importance of the interpreter's mastery of the target language.

This reformulation might be called 'stylistic', without that word having any pejorative or subordinating connotation. It is particularly important because of the cumulative impact of simultaneous interpreting on an audience. If a delegate hears one sentence, or even a two-minute speech, interpreted in a way that makes the interpretation sound like a translation, they probably will not mind too much. But a typical real situation is for a meeting to last for, say, six hours. If delegates are subjected to calque, to French sounding like it should be English, or German sounding like it should be Russian, for several hours, then they will have much more difficulty following a meeting. Indeed, I would contend that in such cases, merely because of the form of the interpretation, there will be a communication gap between speakers and listeners, and the longer the meeting goes on, the wider that gap will grow.

For example, in English a speaker may use subsidiary clauses where the idea is expressed essentially through the use of a verb: 'When the president came to power...', 'After the military junta seized power...', 'Before the president in exile was assassinated...'. It is quite possible to translate all these clauses pretty well word-for-word into French without doing any violence to the French language. But if a French person were speaking freely, without referring to an English original, they would probably choose to express the same ideas through nouns instead of the verbs we find in English, giving literally, 'On the arrival in power of the president...', 'After the taking of power by the military junta...', or 'Before the assassination of the president in exile...'.

Each interpreter should have a feeling for the structures used in their target language and be able to use them naturally irrespective of the source language input. As we have just seen, some languages may prefer more noun-based structures, others more verb-based. Some languages may use passive constructions freely, others nearly never use them. The same thing applies to phrases with deponent verbs. Or we could take the example of the vague term *one*: 'one should do this', 'one has decided that...', etc. In some languages there is no problem using it; in others it sounds too vague or pompous; while in still further languages it is considered too familiar!

By respecting the structures of the target language the interpreter will provide a translation that is convincing and easy to listen to, increasing the audience's comfort of listening and probably maximizing communication. But interpreters may also achieve two other aims. First, they may well make life easier for themselves by avoiding complicated grammar and syntax. For example, there are languages where expressions such as, 'It would be important that we...' or 'It would be necessary that we...' must be followed by subjunctives in the next

clause, and these subjunctives may be in tenses and forms that are rare or difficult for the interpreter to use, particularly under the stress of simultaneous. In
such cases, a reformulation may be used to simplify the verbal forms. You could
reword as 'It would be important/necessary for us to...', thus making it possible
to continue the sentence with a verb in the infinitive. Similarly, interpreters can
avoid being tied in knots when there are a number of interrelationships, such
as 'If you look at the 1996 figures, in column 2, and compare with those of
1995, the net balance of which is given at the foot of column 1, in relation to the
difference between which the percentage is given in column 3, you will see
that...'. Interpreters must not be drawn into this kind of gobbledygook, even if
it is what their delegates say. They will have the greatest difficulty getting it
right, and even if they do succeed there is a fair chance their audience will still
not understand. The audience will be much better served with something as
simple as 'The 1996 figures are in column 2, the 1995 ones in column 1, with
the net balance at the bottom. Column 3 shows the percentage difference between the two. Comparing these, you will see that...'. A last example of making
life easier for oneself, as well as for the audience, is if a speaker uses double or
even triple negatives. If a speaker says, 'There has never been a period in history when people have not asked themselves the question...', the interpreter can
reformulate as 'Throughout history people have always asked themselves the
question...'. The same rule applies to cases where there is not strictly speaking a
double negative but where there are two ideas that may be merged logically into
one. For example, 'The duty suspension cannot be granted unless there is a
proven need for the product on the national market' can become 'The duty suspension can only be granted if there is a proven need...'.

Second, a reformulation that respects the distinctive character of a language
can give an interpretation that renders meaning through syntax. There are languages, including English, where syntax has little or no effect on meaning and
you have to use stress or intonation to indicate what is important in a sentence.
'He painted *the door* blue' may imply I wanted the window frames doing instead; 'He painted the door *blue*' tells us rather that the door should have been
green, or some other colour. But there are other languages, particularly Slavic
languages, where the syntax alone could give us that information. When working into such languages it is particularly important to use reformulation in order
to let the syntax do its work. Moreover, in languages where syntax plays a
greater role, it not only provides meaning within an individual sentence but also
structures a whole speech. One could take the example of Czech, where the
'theme', the reference back to elements already mentioned or known to the listener, tends to be put at the beginning of a sentence, and the 'rheme', the new
information for the listener, which is also generally the point the speaker is
insisting upon, tends to be put at the end of a sentence. Thus, let us suppose a
source language gives:

> Strange behaviour on the part of whales in the southern Atlantic has been observed over a number of years now. A team of marine scientists has come up with a new theory to explain this behaviour. But considerable controversy has arisen in Argentina about the theory.

In syntactic terms (but not as a literal word-for-word translation) this could be reformulated by a Czech interpreter as:

> Whales in the southern Atlantic over a number of years now have been observed behaving strangely. To explain this behaviour [theme] a team of marine scientists has come up with a new theory [rheme]. But about the theory [theme] has arisen in Argentina considerable controversy [rheme].

Reformulating in this way can not only sound better style to a Czech audience but may actually make more sense, thus enhancing the audience's understanding.

We have so far seen that reformulation is important for interpreters in that it enables them to render the ideas of a speaker while respecting the form of expression in the target language. The form of the interpretation is improved. And, as form is content, the content is also improved. But there is another way in which reformulation contributes to the best possible content: it makes word-for-word translation impossible.

As we have stressed repeatedly, the interpreter does not so much ask 'What did the speaker say?' as 'What did the speaker mean?'. When working in consecutive, the interpreter can take a certain intellectual distance from the text of the speaker and will naturally reformulate things in a way appropriate to the target language. But when they are working in simultaneous, the speaker's words will still be ringing in their ears as they interpret, the sentence being interpreted has not even been finished by the speaker, and so the interpreter is much more dependent on the speaker's form of expression. If the syntax of the source language and the target language are compatible, the great temptation is to translate word by word. Sometimes such an approach will work. For example, the English sentence, 'The results that we have observed in our tests must be submitted to the board of directors by December' can be translated into a number of languages without the slightest reformulation. If the vocabulary of the two languages is close as well, as for example between two Romance languages, the temptation is even greater.

The problem is that the word by word approach will work only some of the time. One will inevitably come up against words and expressions that cannot be directly transposed into the target language. And if the interpreter has been following the speaker on a word-for-word basis they will find themselves in an inextricable situation, with a sentence they have begun but do not know how to finish. Worse, the interpreter may slip into loose translations that are merely calque; the interpreter believes they are speaking in the target language but what they are saying is either nonsense or – perhaps worse – a mistranslation. For example, an English-language interpreter might talk about 'the advice taken by the commission' when they mean 'the opinion adopted by the committee'. This is a word-for-word translation from another language which, unfortunately in a way, actually means something, but the meaning is quite different from what the speaker said. It would, if anything, have been better for the interpreter to provide a bad translation that was nonsense, since their delegate would then have been alerted to the problem and could at least have tried to find out what the speaker was saying. It is all too easy with certain language pairs for the interpreter to switch on to a kind of 'automatic pilot' and rattle on quite happily about 'propositions in the ambit of the political orientations established by the conference at the level of ministers' (when they mean 'proposals based on the political guidelines fixed by the ministerial conference'). The problem is aggravated by the fact that some delegates, used to international meetings, adulterate their own use of language. English speakers may litter their speech with Gallicisms, and everyone else tends to use Anglicisms and Americanisms. It is up to the interpreter to resist the temptation to sink into the quagmire of internationalese where meanings become increasingly blurred, even if delegates do not resist that temptation.

A subsidiary advantage of not working in a word-for-word way is that one can obviate the difficulty of what we might call 'multi-translations'. An interpreter may be working from a number of passive languages, say three. The meeting is about cooperation between Mediterranean riparian states. If the interpreter is too dependent on the form of expression in the source languages, following slavishly the exact turns of phrase, then from one language they may say, 'the Mediterranean shore countries', from another 'the Mediterranean basin countries', and from the third 'the countries neighbouring the Mediterranean'. In all cases they mean the same thing, but they put it differently each time because of the influence of the source language. That is what we term the problem of 'multi-translation'.

There is nothing wrong with an interpreter having a rich and varied vocabulary. On the contrary. But the interpreter should be able to use that vocabulary as they see fit, and also remain consistent when appropriate. If the interpreter's terminology varies all the time, or perhaps if it suddenly changes after an hour's debate, their audience may be misled into thinking the interpreter is genuinely talking about something different. The audience cannot be expected to understand that the interpreter's form of expression has changed because it is following the vagaries of the source languages, and that one term is used because it comes from a Romance language and a different one because it comes from a Germanic language. Taking more intellectual distance from the text and reformulating should make it possible to avoid this problem.

A further advantage of reformulation is that it enables the interpreter to deal with words they do not know. A word unknown to an interpreter may mean a word they recognize and know the meaning of in the source language but do not know how to express in the target language. It may also mean a word that is unknown to the interpreter in the source language. If someone were to say to the interpreter, out of context, 'What does X mean?' the interpreter would have to admit that they had never heard the word before and could therefore not answer.

It is this latter case that is usually meant when non-interpreters ask interpreters the inevitable question: 'What do you do when you come up against a word you don't know?'. This question has to be dealt with head-on somewhere in this book, and it is the technique of reformulation that makes it possible to give the fullest reply.

When we discussed consecutive interpreting, the eventuality of the unknown word was mentioned but commented on only briefly. In consecutive the interpreter hears the whole speech before being called upon to interpret; they thus have a number of possibilities open to them. They may grasp the exact meaning of the word in question from the context of the speech. They may grasp the general meaning of the word and be in a position to give a reasonable rendering of it, even if the translation they give is not the exact dictionary translation, or perhaps provide a generic term rather than the specific one used by the speaker. They may be able to express the idea used by the speaker without having recourse to the unknown word. They may ask the speaker for a clarification at the end of the speech before they start their interpretation. If they are lucky, particularly in a technical meeting, there may even be a delegate who knows the technical vocabulary in two or more languages and who can provide the right term for the interpreter. In the interactive context of a consecutive interpretation such problems can usually be sorted out.

Yet the question often put by non-interpreters in relation to simultaneous is quite understandable and justified. In the middle of simultaneous, you do not have the whole speech to provide context, you cannot interrupt a speaker or wait until the end to put a question; above all, if you are in mid-sentence and have to translate a word in that sentence you have never heard before, how do you cope?

First, although the simultaneous interpreter does not have the whole context, they do have some context. They have the overall context of the meeting, and of course the specific context of a speaker's comments up to the point at which the unknown word occurs. The worst thing that can happen from this point of view is that a speaker begins by saying, 'I should now like to talk about hops', and the interpreter does not know the word *hops*. With no context to work from, how does one react? To be frank, this kind of occurrence in an interpreter's real working life is so rare as to be not worth worrying about. In the artificial context of an interpreting exam, at a school or with an international organization, such a problem may arise: a speech may be given on any topic, without warning to the candidate, who might then be caught out. But in a meeting, you normally know what the subject of the meeting is; the interpreter arrives shortly before the beginning of the meeting and may look over the agenda, consult documents or revise the documentation provided in advance. Later the same day they may find themselves facing terminological problems relating, say, to the processes hops are subjected to for making beer. But the chances that they will be faced with lexical problems at the beginning of proceedings with no context at all are minimal.

Thus the simultaneous interpreter, like the consecutive interpreter, does have context, even if it is rather less. A precondition if one wishes to benefit from such context is rather obviously that the interpreter must follow the meeting, even when they are not interpreting; listening to the delegations speaking your target language can be particularly useful, as they may provide the target-language terminology you may be lacking at the beginning of the meeting. Second, the interpreter is not really following 'just behind' the speaker. If the interpreter *were* just behind the speaker, then at the least obstacle they would stumble over. But if, as we have seen above, the interpreter has taken a short 'distance' from the speaker, they will have time to react to any unknown word that crops up. Third, and most important, the interpreter is reformulating. If one tackles interpreting as a sequence of lexical correspondences to be established, then once a correspondence is unavailable the whole system will break down.

For example, let's assume the text to be interpreted is:

> To diagnose such a throat disorder a general practitioner is not enough.
> The patient should be referred to an otorhinolaryngologist.

If the interpreter is doing this by finding lexical equivalents in the target language and does not know the last word, then disaster threatens. If, however, the interpreter works from context, has sufficient distance from the speaker and uses reformulation, then the possibilities open to them are little different from those in consecutive. The interpreter can work out, for the example above, what kind of a doctor is being referred to. They may know what is meant and use a less technical term such as *ear, nose and throat specialist*. They may have only a vague sense of what is meant but from the beginning of the sentence deduce that the patient needs a 'throat specialist'. They could even fall back on a generic term and simply say the patient needs to see a 'specialist'.

Above all, with reformulation you can express ideas without ever having to use an unknown word, provided, of course, you understand the speaker's meaning. Let's assume that government funding to universities is being discussed. A delegate asks:

> Is the new funding for research to be considered as counterpart funding?
> If so, what is the share of the co-funding expected from the universities?
> Are they expected to match government funding exactly? And do they
> have to provide their counterpart from their own funds, or can industry
> contributions to research projects at a university be used for matching
> funds?

The interpreter does not know the term 'counterpart funding' (which in this
context means funding from one body, here the government, provided on the
condition that an other body also provides funding, usually to the same amount
as the first body). They therefore begin with a non-committal 'How is the new
funding for research to be considered?'. Then as the penny drops and they gradually see what the speaker is driving at, they might continue:

> What share of co-funding is expected of universities? Do they have to
> provide exactly the same amount as the government, *if there must be co-*
> *funding? Must universities co-finance*, and if so must they use their own
> funds, or can industry contributions to their research work also be used?

The words in italics here show the stage at which the interpreter grasps the idea
fully and retrieves their initial omission – due to the non-committal beginning –
by building the relative question back in. At no stage has the interpreter talked
of 'counterpart funds', but the questions put are essentially the same as those
put by the speaker, and the interpreter's delegate will now be in a position to
give answers to those questions.

A last word is necessary on the question of words interpreters do not know.
There are many resources available to an interpreter to deal with the problem.
Besides those mentioned above, you should remember that in simultaneous an
interpreter should not be alone in the booth. Their colleague may be able to help
out: they may know the word or can look it up in a glossary, or if they cannot
help directly they might be able to slip into another booth to ask for assistance.
With modern technology it is also increasingly possible for interpreters to call
up terminology from data bases in the booth. But when all is said and done,
there will still be occasions when an interpreter is confronted with a word they
do not know. It may be that there is no way of getting round the problem, however much technique the interpreter has, without betraying the speaker, and the
interpreter judges that the word is too important for it to be omitted. In such a
case, as a matter of professional ethics, the same rule applies as for consecutive
interpretation: the simultaneous interpreter should be honest and inform their
audience that there is a word or expression that they cannot translate. The audience can then decide whether they feel it is important. They may not care less,
in which case there is no harm done, particularly as this will happen very rarely,
provided the interpreter has the right technique. If, however, delegates decide

that they wish to seek clarification from the speaker, they will be grateful to the interpreter for their honesty and for having contributed to mutual understanding.

Thus far we have stated the various advantages, both stylistic and in terms of enhancing content, arising from use of reformulation. But there is a more fundamental point that should be made about the interpreter's overall intellectual approach. The fact that an interpreter is using reformulation is a sign that they are doing their work properly. The interpreter has to understand, but then also to analyze and process the information they have understood. If translation is done systematically in a word-for-word way, the interpreter cannot be analyzing the ideas enough. Such a method will induce intellectual laziness, words becoming a convenient prop for the interpreter who can then continue their way without trying to get at the ideas behind the words. At best, the interpreter is analyzing the language of the speaker, not the ideas.

The natural product of discourse analysis must be that when a speech is re-expressed, particularly if it is re-expressed in a different language, it will be formulated differently. An interpreter who analyzes properly must, by definition, use reformulation.

Now that the need for reformulation has been established and some examples of its advantages have been given, we can ask how the interpreter actually sets about reformulating.

First, reformulation should come about as a matter of course if the interpreter adopts the approach we described above concerning the moment at which to start speaking. If the interpreter is lagging slightly behind the speaker and concentrates on starting their own sentence in a way which will enable them to finish it, there is already a fair chance that their text will diverge, in its form, from that of the speaker.

Second, even if the speaker begins a sentence in an unproblematic way from the point of view of the interpreter, the interpreter should still be cautious about just rushing in and following the speaker's line. 'Unproblematic' here means that the speaker's sentence makes it possible for the interpreter to finish their own sentences, even if they follow the syntax of the speaker, and that there are no particular lexical, conceptual or translative difficulties for the interpreter. Even though the beginning of a speaker's comments may be unproblematic, they might become more difficult to cope with, and the interpreter could regret having simply followed the speaker down their road. One way of developing autonomy is to see whether you can start a sentence in a different way from the speaker. If the beginning of the sentence is different, even if strictly speaking it did not need to be, then the sentence as a whole will enjoy greater freedom in relation to the original.

This technique in particular can be practised by students of interpretation: in simultaneous they can try to force themselves to begin all of their sentences differently from the speaker. This can be good practice, particularly as students tend to seek the other extreme, that is, following the speaker too closely. The exercise should get them into the good habit of not following the speaker automatically. However, I must stress that this is not what we recommend professional interpreters to do. Students should certainly be cautious about following a speaker too closely and must thus be aware of the possibilities of expressing the speaker's ideas differently. But on the other hand, interpreters should not force themselves into a straitjacket by not allowing themselves ever to follow the speaker's structure. There are times when the only sensible translation is one that follows the speaker very closely, when any attempt to put the idea differently would involve torturing the target language. Systematic reformulation, pursued as an end in itself, would be very tiring, is far from necessary, and would sometimes be counterproductive. Reformulation, in its various forms, is one of the most useful tools the simultaneous interpreter has. But it is still only a tool, a means to an end.

Third, reformulation becomes a kind of second nature to interpreters as they listen to ideas and express them freely in their own words. Yet this is only possible if the interpreter is able to use their target language(s) in a rich and varied way. The interpreter must therefore keep fully in touch with their target language(s), in particular through reading widely. This means reading the press, to keep abreast of both current affairs and topical terminology; publications for the popularization of technical subjects such as medical research, information technology, and so on; and well written general literature (history books, novels, etc.), to broaden vocabulary and improve style. An interpreter who is cut off from their target language, perhaps living in a country of another language and not reading widely, will be stunted in their work, and in particular will be less able to take stylistic liberties in reformulation.

Finally, there are a number of specific examples of reformulation that can be given but which merit mention as techniques for simultaneous interpreting in their own right. The subsequent points of this section will therefore present various techniques, although you will soon see that many of them are variations on the theme of reformulation.

The Salami Technique

In simultaneous interpreters need to be able to express themselves in short, simple sentences, for the reasons explained above. Speakers, however, may – indeed, usually do – use long, complicated sentences. The logical conclusion is that the interpreter must divide up the speaker's sentences into a number of short, self-contained ones and then link them as appropriate. Take the following sentence, which is reasonably typical of much that interpreters hear in meetings:

> Japan, in the light of the ruling of the international panel, and following the non-payment of the compensation by the American steel exporters,

which the US authorities have not forced them to pay, despite their legal
obligations and the assurances they have given, has decided to act unilat-
erally, which they are perfectly entitled to in the case of non-compliance
with an international panel ruling – and that is the case here – by impos-
ing punitive duties on the import of certain flat products, although long
ones should remain unaffected, at least for the immediate future.

This is the kind of spoken language that comes quite naturally to delegates.
Other delegates listening directly, not through interpretation, understand perfectly well in context, despite the difficulties of the text. There is a grammatical
error; the subject of the main clause is separated from the main verb by four
lines; and there is at least technically an ambiguity in the third and fourth lines:
'which the US authorities have not forced them to pay, despite their legal obligations and the assurances they have given'. It is clear that *them* refers to the
steel exporters, but who, after that, do *'their* legal obligations' and 'assurances
they have given' refer to? Grammatically, it could be the steel exporters. But in
fact, it means the US authorities. This is all well and good for the delegate, who
knows the context and who merely has to soak up the information. But the
interpreter has the acoustic difficulty of speaking at the same time and the intellectual difficulty of sorting out the sentence, in all probability with a less perfect
understanding of the background.

So what should the interpreter do? The answer is to divide the one long
sentence up into a number of shorter ones. As this is 'slicing up' a sentence,
rather as one might cut slices of a salami, the process is generally referred to,
somewhat inelegantly, as the 'salami technique'.

Applying the approach discussed above for deciding when to begin speak-
ing, the interpreter can begin when the speaker has reached *international panel*.
They should not begin with a reference to Japan, as they have no idea as to how
Japan is to fit into the sentence. They will therefore begin with something like,
'The international panel has made its ruling'. This way, they may arrive at some-
thing like the following:

> The international panel has made its ruling. Compensation has not been
> paid by the American steel exporters. The US authorities have not obliged
> them to pay, although they have legal obligations and have given assur-
> ances in this respect. So Japan has decided to react unilaterally. It is quite
> entitled to do so, as the ruling of the international panel has not been
> respected. It will impose punitive duties on imports of some flat prod-
> ucts. Long products should not be immediately affected.

The interpreter has made seven sentences out of one. Five of those sentences
have only one clause. The two other sentences are barely more complicated.

The interpreter's overall text is slightly shorter than the original, and the way the different sentences or clauses have been related to one another has generally been simplified and streamlined. That is the kind of interpretation that interpreters themselves can cope with, and which the audience will find easy to follow. Of course, I do not pretend that this 'interpretation' cannot be improved upon: it is merely one illustration of a technique, and, like other illustrations in this book, is limited by the fact that it 'interprets' from English into English.

You might notice that Japan is mentioned by the interpreter only about halfway through the passage. In this particular example it may be easy to remember *Japan*, especially in the context of a real meeting. However, a notion that has to be held back when interpreting and mentioned only two or three sentences later might not always be so easy to recall, particularly as the interpreter has to continue directing their attention to whatever comes next in the speech. A simple thing to do, if the need should arise, is to jot down the word (for the example above the interpreter need not even write down *Japan* in full; the letter J would probably suffice). Then when the interpreter reaches the main verb they can, if necessary, look at their note-pad to remind themselves of the subject of that verb. It should not be forgotten, particularly by conference organizers and those responsible for catering for interpreters' practical needs, that conference interpreters, even in simultaneous, should always have writing materials available in the booth.

The salami technique is particularly useful when working from languages that have a natural tendency to long, complicated sentences, particularly those that can have Russian doll-like structures, with one subordinate clause fitting in another one, which in turn fits into a main clause (such as the so-called *Schachtelsätze* in German). For example, the English sentence:

> We have tried to get into contact with the photographer who had identified the man seen bringing assistance to the injured on the scene of this serious accident.

With German word order this could be:

> We have tried with the photographer, who the man [accusative case], who on the scene of this serious accident was seen, as he to the injured assistance brought, had identified, to get into contact.

If the interpreter's job is to put this into English, how on earth do they set about it? One cannot wait until the end of the entire sentence to say something, but it is difficult to know how to finish a sentence at all for a long time. One can hardly make something out of the first six words, and thereafter the speaker starts two separate subordinate clauses, the second one being subordinate not to the main clause, but to the first subordinate. This is a circumstance where the interpreter has to weigh up the pros and cons of waiting until they are totally sure they can finish their sentence. If they have the courage to wait until *was seen* and have time to fit all the rest in afterwards, all the better. That is the ideal solution. But we do not live in an ideal world, and others may prefer to run the risk of starting after *the man, who....* At this stage, the interpreter will have recognized the beginning of the doubly subordinate clause, knows from the grammar that *the man* in question is the subject of that clause, and has good enough hopes of making something coherent of the sentence to warrant starting speaking. A particular reason for starting to speak at that moment is that the speaker, however perverse, is unlikely to build in a triply subordinate clause, that is, one that is subordinate to the clause beginning 'the man, who...'.

Whichever of these two options the interpreter takes, their first words are likely to be 'A man was seen at this serious accident'. Using the salami technique, the interpreter's output can now become:

> A man was seen at this serious accident. He was helping the injured. He has been identified by a photographer. We have tried to get into contact with the photographer.

Once the interpreter gets going, they are able to take in and interpret the extra information the speaker is giving. At the same time they can catch up on the elements from the beginning of the sentence initially left out, building them back into the interpretation. They are able to do this in a form that is easy for them to produce as it creates no intrinsic grammatical difficulties.

Not only can the salami technique help with such Russian doll-like sentences with subordinate clauses, but it can be of assistance when an entire subordinate clause is placed before the noun it refers to and is used in an adjectival function. For example, in English one would say, 'the man who(m) the photographer identified'. To take the example of German again, it is possible, in that language, to translate the English word-for-word. But it is also possible to say, 'the by the photographer identified man'.

Thus, if we change the above example slightly, and it is no longer the photographer but the man in question that we wish to contact, a German sentence might run:

> We have tried, with the by the photographer identified man, who at this serious accident was seen, as he to the injured provided assistance, to get into contact.

This is an easier sentence to interpret than the previous one. By *identified man*, the interpreter can already start, having enough material to provide a complete sentence of their own. Then they can divide the speaker's sentence up into:

> The photographer has identified a man, who was seen at this serious accident. He was helping the injured. We have tried to contact him.

Efficiency in Reformulation

One of the main formal objectives of the simultaneous interpreter is efficiency of expression. The interpreter is constantly under time pressure, having to produce their interpretation at the same speed as the speaker, but with the added burden of having to translate and not knowing where they are going. Provided speakers know what they want to say and are not deliberately slow speakers, the interpreter will always have to work out techniques for keeping up. Every second can count, and it is important to express oneself as succinctly as possible. This is so much the case that sometimes an interpreter's choice will go to one form of expression because it is the form that contains the least syllables.

The need to be able to reformulate so as to express oneself efficiently exists for all languages, but it should be noted that for some languages it is more acute than for others. English is by nature a dense, succinct language. English-language interpreters are lucky in that this often gives them an inbuilt advantage, which makes them the envy of colleagues working into other languages. Interpreters working into Romance languages often have an uphill struggle in that their language forces them to use, say, fifty percent more words than a given source language to say the same thing.

One way of being succinct is to make use of a speaker's reference to previous comments in the meeting. Let's assume that in a meeting on international civil law with a number of national delegations, one of them, say the Belgian delegation, has asked a question about the legal means open to a landlord to sue a former tenant who is of a different nationality and has returned to their home country. It is clear that all the delegations present know that this is the Belgian question. Then, another delegation takes the floor and begins, 'On the Belgian question concerning...' and proceeds to repeat the entire Belgian question. The interpreter may then, if they feel it is necessary to save time, simply say, 'I should like to say something about the Belgian question'. Alternatively, they may feel this would leave an excessively long silence and give their audience the impression that the interpretation is woefully incomplete. In that case, they could choose to summarize the Belgian question very simply. The only case in which the interpreter is really obliged to interpret the entire repetition of the Belgian question is if they deduce that the speaker from the other delegation, who is not speaking the same language as the Belgian delegate, is repeating the question in order to check that they have understood it correctly, and will take silence from the Belgian delegation as meaning that they have.

Of course, this kind of technique works only if the reference to the Belgian delegation enlightens the audience. If in a large gathering a speaker says, 'On the question of the gentleman at the back with a beard, concerning...', few people in the room will identify the gentleman in question, and even fewer will be able to relate him to his question. There, the interpreter must be complete, and if anything is to be omitted at all, it is rather the reference to the person who put the question than the question itself.

Examples where one can make reference back crop up all the time in an interpreter's work. They may be much smaller than the one above and concern just a few words. For example, an international trade tribunal is part of the object of a discussion. Some delegations keep repeating scrupulously, 'the international trade tribunal'. Provided this is the only tribunal in the debate and there is no risk of confusion, it is legitimate for the interpreter to say, 'the tribunal'. Such tactics can save precious seconds, and if used as part of a consistent strategy can make all the difference between keeping up with a speaker and not keeping up.

The tactic just described is based on the principle of exploiting cognitive knowledge shared by the interpreter and their audience. The interpreter knows the knowledge is shared because of what has happened during the meeting (which, incidentally, is another good reason for following a meeting even if one is not 'on mike'). But an interpreter may also exploit shared cognitive knowledge coming from outside the meeting. Let's imagine, for example, that the President of the United States has made an extremely important speech in Montreal on the future of pan-American relations. It has been in the news everywhere and is highly topical; everyone should know about it. If a delegate chooses to say 'the American President's speech in Montreal on the future of pan-American relations', the interpreter can express that satisfactorily as 'the American President's Montreal speech'. If they are lucky, in context they may even be able to pare this down to 'the Montreal speech'; why not?

The interpreter can also save a lot of time by referring to documents, organizations, etc. in an abbreviated or simplified form, provided this form is clear for the audience and is accepted usage. Thus the speaker's 'International Atomic Energy Agency' can become the 'Vienna Agency', the 'Treaty establishing the European Economic Community' can become the 'EEC Treaty' or the 'Treaty of Rome'.

The interpreter should seek economy of expression everywhere. This means, first, removing all useless filler words such as *really*, *actually*, *well*, etc. (unless these words are being used in their strict, primary sense). These are words to be kept in store for desperately slow speakers where one needs to fill in the silence a bit, and even then they should be used only with parsimony.

Second, it means not taking rhetorical precautions with one's audience by adding phrases such as *so to speak/say*, *if you like*, *if you see what I mean*. Such phrases are a waste of time and will only give the impression that the interpreter is not totally sure about their own interpretation (which is usually the case when they use such expressions).

Third, unnecessary repetitions are banned. Speakers may deliberately repeat notions, with synonyms or near-synonyms, to make a point particularly forcefully. If that is the case, the interpreter has to repeat with the speaker (as mentioned on consecutive). But most repetition on the part of delegates is gratuitous. In particular, in some languages and for a certain kind of delegate a triptych of adjectives or verbs seems to be considered the acme of good style. This gives sentences such as, 'This proposal needs to be carefully studied, examined and analyzed'. Other speakers are tautologous, talking of 'innovating with a new initiative' and so on. Interpreters should tidy up such language. And of course, if such things are not in the original, the interpreter should not introduce them into their own version.

Fourth, interpreters must be generally vigilant about their own form of expression and choose the shortest form, where possible. *As far as ... is concerned* can usually be replaced by *On ...*. Or again, *We must do this in conjunction/ cooperation with one another* can as a general rule be simply, *We must do this together*. The list of examples is endless, whatever the target language, and so are the consequent time savings. Interpreters should also have an eye for a shortcut. For example, a delegate may talk about 'the coordination meeting to exchange our impressions after the Helsinki conference'. That may seem natural to the speaker, and there is no earthly reason why the interpreter should not translate the phrase more or less literally. But if the interpreter is alert and grasps what is being referred to, they may interpret the whole phrase as 'the debriefing on Helsinki'.

Fifth, interpreters should be prepared to provide a 'no frills' interpretation where this is appropriate. This means an interpretation where the speaker's verbosity is ironed out. Here we take verbosity to be a different problem from repetition and tautology, but the interpreter's response remains the same. If an announcement is made to the press corps to the effect that 'you will have the opportunity or putting direct oral questions to the Minister with a view to his informing you about the situation currently prevailing in the negotiations', the interpreter could inform the press corps that 'you will be able to ask the Minister questions about the state of the negotiations'. The ultimate pruning of verbosity would be if a chairperson asks a delegate, 'Can you agree?' and the delegate answers, 'I have to inform you that my position on this question means that my answer is in the negative'. The interpretation of the answer may well be 'No'.

This last technique is one that can help interpreters make considerable time savings. However, a word of warning is necessary. It may be that a delegate wishes to adopt a literary or rhetorical style with certain oratorical effects. If that is the case the interpreter should make an effort to respect the style. Second, it may be that a speaker is trying to be particularly diplomatic. Then, the interpreter must make sure that no nuance is lost. To return to the previous example, let us assume the answer is, 'Unfortunately, Mr Chairman, I have to inform you that for the moment my instructions are that my delegation's position remains negative'. This can most definitely not be interpreted as 'no'. There is the idea 'unfortunately', which expresses regret about the refusal. Then the speaker says the all-important words 'for the moment'. This holds out hope that in future the position will change. Third, the speaker refers to their instructions and says 'my delegation', thus personally distancing themselves somewhat from the official position. The first answer we cited really meant 'no'. This answer means, 'not now, but I think I can get my authorities to change their minds'. The subtlety of the latter answer has to be recognized by the interpreter, reading between the lines, and then it has to be brought out in the interpretation by following the speaker more closely, although even there it will not be necessary to repeat every word they use.

Simplification

Most interpreters at some time in their career find themselves faced with the task of interpreting highly technical material. For such speeches it may be desirable, or even necessary, to simplify a speech, and that for two reasons. First, it may be that the speech is so technical that the interpreter, despite their best efforts to prepare a meeting and despite documentation made available to them, just cannot render all of the technical details. In such a case, they must at least try to save the essentials by simplification. Second, the speaker may be talking over the heads of their audience. The interpreter may very well be able to cope with the speech, but a faithful rendering would just leave the audience confused. Let's begin with this second type of case.

I am aware that this point is controversial and may shock colleagues who feel it is the interpreter's first duty to be as faithful as possible to the speaker. Such colleagues may argue it is the speaker's fault if they speak in a way that cannot be understood by their audience, and it is not up to the interpreter to palliate the problem. Moreover, for an interpreter to judge an audience unfit to listen to an unsimplified version of a speech may seem at the very least patronizing, not to say arrogant.

These points are valid, which is why deliberate simplification on the part of the interpreter is a technique to be used sparingly and carefully. But I would argue that an interpreter's first duty is not so much to be faithful to the speaker's words come what may, but to maximize communication.

If, for example, a group of teenagers is being provided information on the Common Agricultural Policy of the European Community, they need to understand the explanations they receive. 'If the CIF price of produce at the Community border is below the guideline price as determined under the Common Market Organization, then a levy, which is not a tariff duty, is imposed', is the kind of thing layman youngsters will find impenetrable, unless most of the terms are explained by the speaker. The interpreter may find it better to say to the audience, 'If farm produce comes into the Community at a price below the official Community market price, a special agricultural levy is imposed' (which could be seen as a particular form of simplification: interpreting unfamiliar jargon into everyday language).

Such communication gaps may be bridged not just in the case of young people. Simplification can apply to any case of an expert talking in the wrong register to laymen. Take a nuclear scientist explaining to political decision makers the safety characteristics of different kinds of reactors. On high temperature reactors they explain:

> The core is made of a graphite matrix entrapping the refractory fuel particles, which are 1mm spheres with a nucleus of uranium or plutonium oxide or carbide, coated with polycarbon or silicon carbide to separate the fissile matter of the particles.

Assuming the interpreter has some kind of training on nuclear reactors, or at least has been well briefed and is therefore in a position to cope with this, they can explain to their delegates in a simpler way. They could say:

> The core is made of graphite. This entraps the fuel particles. The particles, with a core of uranium or plutonium, are in turn coated with polycarbon or silicon carbide [or even, if the interpreter feels this detail is meaningless to their delegates, 'with another substance'], to separate the fissile matter.

It is not that the delegates are so stupid or ignorant that they cannot cope with notions such as 'uranium oxide', but their overall understanding of what the expert is driving at will probably gain from a streamlined presentation: if they are not themselves scientists the full text may leave them 'blinded by science', and they may miss the main point.

Simplification is also a technique to help the interpreter when the going gets too tough for them. It may sound like a logical impossibility, in that it can be argued that simplification is possible only if in the first place one has understood; how can you simplify if you do not know what you are simplifying? However, I feel that an interpreter can identify the essence of a statement or a question, and convey it, without understanding all of the details expressed by a speaker; or, they may have understood but do not necessarily have all the target-language vocabulary at their fingertips to express everything quickly enough.

For example, if a chemist talks about the usefulness of metal leaching for different metals, they may explain the following:

> Trace elements may be silicious or extrasilicious. Silicious elements, such as titanium or chromium, are linked to the silicate network as primary constituents of the crystal mesh or by diadochic replacement, and so have low chemical mobility. Extrasilicious elements, such as copper and lead, lie outside the network in simple compounds, such as oxides, and are therefore much more mobile.

Here the audience is composed of chemists, so if there were not the language barrier they would understand everything. The problem is that the poor interpreter does not understand and does not have all the vocabulary in their target language. In such a case, the interpreter must ask, again, what the speaker is driving at, and in particular must ask themselves that question in context. Here, the discussion is about the metals for which leaching is worthwhile. Mobile elements will be easier to leach than immobile ones. And the interpreter learns from the speaker that silicious means 'immobile' and extrasilicious means 'mobile'. That must therefore figure in the interpretation. One would not necessarily have to prune back the interpretation so drastically, but one could convey the essential message by saying:

> Trace elements may be found in silicates or outside them. Those in silicates, like titanium and chromium, are bound into the silicate. So they are not very mobile. Those outside it, like copper and lead, are found elsewhere in simple compounds [such as oxides], and so are much more mobile.

Sadly, a fair amount of information has been lost, and the interpreter does not use the correct technical terms. But assuming the speaker is developing an argument to the effect that we should concentrate on extrasilicious metals for leaching, then the other delegates will have followed and the interpreter will essentially have done their job.

Such simplification can be particularly important if there is a direct dialogue between two participants in a meeting, with the one asking questions of the other. For example, in a meeting on product liability for consumer protection, one legal expert asks another:

> If the commercial guarantee is no longer applicable and no legal remedy is available for the buyer in relation to the producer under the legal guarantee, because of problems of burden of proof and the statute of limitation in the producer's country, can a product liability legal guarantee be invoked against the seller in the seller's country if it is a different country?

Let's assume the interpreter has difficulties understanding and/or expressing both 'burden of proof' and 'statute of limitations'. The interpreter can still identify the main notions in the question: the commercial guarantee does not apply; the legal guarantee will not work in relation to the producer; can the legal guarantee then be invoked in relation to the seller? To provide an answer to the question the interpreter's client must understand at least that. The interpreter could thus provide sufficient interpretation even if the words *because of problems of burden of proof and the statute of limitation in the producer's country* are interpreted as *because of technical legal problems in the producer's country*. The whole, simplified interpretation could become:

> Let us assume the commercial guarantee no longer applies. The buyer can take no legal action against the producer under the legal guarantee, because of technical legal problems in the producer's country. Can they use the product liability legal guarantee against the seller, if the seller is in a different country?

Again, the interpreter has definitely lost something in the interpretation, but at least now their delegate can give a useful answer to the question put to them.

With examples such as this we should not forget that interpreting is also a percentages game. A perfectionist would make a supreme effort to interpret even the problematic passage. But in practice the upshot would probably be that they would spend so much time and effort on it that the more important element, the question at the end, would be less satisfactorily interpreted. The interpreter must know how to sacrifice the less important to the more important (which also implies they are carrying out a sufficient analysis of the speech to identify what is important, and what is less important).

Generalization

It may also be that an interpreter does not feel technical simplification is necessary for either of the reasons mentioned above, but that to save time, perhaps with a very fast speaker, a number of specific items mentioned can be expressed in one generic term.

A speaker could say, 'People take it for granted now to have a fridge and a freezer, the dishwasher and the washing machine with a spin dryer, a cooker and a vacuum cleaner'. If the speaker is going at a rate of knots and the detail of this list is irrelevant, the interpreter can generalize (in the sense of using a generic term) and interpret, 'People take it for granted now to have all household electrical appliances'.

Again, this technique should be used only where appropriate. If a speaker gives a list where each element is significant, then the interpreter must do their best to reproduce the list. One does not want to be in the situation of the inter-preter who gave up on a list of chemicals only to hear the chairperson of the meeting say (with a smile), 'Yes, but I must inform the interpreter that "various other chemicals" is not quite enough'.

Omission (Under Duress) and Fast Speakers

Sometimes an interpreter will be under duress because of the technicity of a subject, because of the mode of expression of a speaker, because the speaker is too fast, or a mixture of these factors. The interpreter finds that neither simplifi-cation nor generalization help. The only way to keep afloat is to omit things.

In such circumstances there are two comments that can be made. First, the interpreter must carry on making their analysis of the speech so that they keep in the essential elements and miss out only what is illustrative or in some other way accessory (such as asides, digressions, etc.). This analysis is based on ex-actly the same principles as described for consecutive interpretation.

The second comment is that in order to make this analysis interpreters must give themselves a bit of time and have sufficient intellectual distance from the original. If the problem is the technicity of the subject or an abstruse or complex mode of expression on the part of the speaker, the interpreter will automatically be devoting a large share of their energy to understanding and analyzing. But even if the problem is the sheer speed of the speaker, then the interpreter must proceed in the same way. The last thing the interpreter should do is enter into a race with the speaker. The interpreter will get caught in a vicious circle: racing behind the speaker, they will have less time to analyse meaning and less time to decide how to express it. As they have less time to analyze they will be more and more dependent on the words the speaker uses. Having less time to decide how to express themselves, their own mode of expression will become increas-ingly sloppy. The overall result will be an interpretation which progressively becomes a poorly expressed word-for-word translation.

On the contrary, with a fast speaker, the interpreter should take some dis-tance, analyze fully, and see how they can use every technique – the salami technique, simplifying, generalizing, general economy of expression, and where necessary omission – to convey as much as possible of the speaker's meaning in as few syllables as possible. There are few things more impressive for an interpreter's audience than to be aware that another delegate is going at their speech hammer and tongues and to hear their interpreter stating things calmly, clearly and collectedly.

Here we must comment more generally on the problem of fast speakers and professional ethics. Different scenarios are possible. In a meeting where par-ticipants speak freely, one or more speakers may just happen to be fast. They are unlikely to be so fast as to be impossible for an interpreter, but if they are really problematic the interpreter may speak through the microphone to request that their delegates ask the speakers in question to go a little slower. Usually this has an impact on the speaker for about thirty seconds, and then they reaccelerate to their normal pace. If that is the case the interpreter should not keep on insisting to their delegates; they must just make the best of a bad job.

Things are quite different when it comes to a speaker who is reading a text at speed. Ideally, the text should be made available to the interpreters before the meeting so that they can prepare it. If that is not the case, however, the speech should be made available at least during the meeting so the interpreters can refer to it at the relevant moment. If an interpreter finds themselves with a text they received about two minutes before the speaker begins, such that they had no time to prepare it, they should use it particularly to identify specific references to proper names, technical terms, and numbers in whatever form they come (dates, statistics, reference documents, etc.). It is these elements that create the most difficulty when a speaker is very fast. It is not necessarily useful to read the speech in the written text word-for-word as the speaker pronounces it. Trying to read in this way can distract the interpreter's concentration from the oral text and can create confusion if the speaker diverges from their written text (which is often the case), such that the interpreter expends mental effort on trying to reconcile the written and spoken versions. However, if the interpreter concentrates hard on listening to the speaker, using the written text to follow approximately where the speaker is and to pick out specific problematic elements such as those mentioned above, then they have a good chance of providing the best interpretation.

The worst situation is when the interpreter has no text at all. A speaker who then reads a text at speed can be quite impossible to interpret, particularly as written texts tend to be more dense and more succinctly expressed than the comments of people speaking freely. The interpreter will have little margin for using techniques such as simplification, generalization or omission of non-essential items. They should of course do their best to interpret whatever is thrown at them, but it is a good thing to warn the audience that the interpreter does not have the written version of the text being presented. It may make a delegate interrupt the speaker and persuade the organizers to give the interpreters a copy. Even if they do not, at least the audience is forewarned that the interpreter is working in circumstances that do not allow an optimal level of interpreting. Then, if the interpreter can cope, all the better. But if the speech is really downright impossible without any supporting documentation – for example the presentation of epidemiological research with mention of little known geographical regions where the research took place, technical, medical terminology, and a detailed statistical analysis of all the data gathered – then the interpreter is not just entitled, but honour-bound, to tell their audience that it is impossible and to stop interpreting. An interpreter should never be forced into a situation where, because of bad organisation, it is materially impossible for them to provide even a semblance of a decent service.

Summarizing and Recapitulation

Having looked at a number of ways the interpreter edits the original in order to improve the interpretation, or in some cases to make an interpretation possible, we should also be aware that there are times when, in order to ensure full understanding on the part of the audience, the interpreter should not edit, but on the contrary add things.

First, an interpreter may wish to summarize or recapitulate what a speaker has already said, and what they themselves have already interpreted, if they feel the audience may have failed to grasp the point. It should be noted that 'summarize' is not being used here in the sense of providing a summary that replaces the full text. It is a summary that is added to the full text, recapitulating the main idea. Nor should it be felt that such a technique has to be used to cover up for the interpreter's own shortcomings. It is quite possible to use this technique, if one has time, to clarify what is unclear because of the speaker.

For example, a chairperson may say:

> The question is whether a legal instrument, and by legal I mean of course also something that could be administrative or just a rule, but anyway something which we would consider legal, although you'd have to think about how to enforce it afterwards, and who would enforce it? There we'd have to look at the question of competence. Or should we just leave it up to industry to exercise voluntary restraint, which is what they want, although they want it, perhaps, precisely because they don't want to be policed, but then again we must bear in mind what our international competitors are doing in this field. I don't know what you think. I'd be interested in hearing your ideas.

That, despite its incoherence, is a question that can be understood by a delegate listening in the same language; they would have an idea of what to comment upon. But much of the chair's reasoning is expressed only implicitly in their words, and an interpreter could justifiably feel that through the filter of translation their audience would not be able to see the wood for the trees. At the end they could thus sum up by asking clearly: 'Are you in favour of a binding legal instrument or a system of voluntary restraint?'. Then the delegates would be sure to know what to comment upon.

Explanation

Second, as in consecutive, interpreters may be faced with notions, cultural and institutional references, and so on, that have no direct equivalent in the target language and which ideally should therefore be explained to the audience. The problem is that this takes time, and the interpreter may not feel that they have that time available. Clearly, if an interpreter cannot fit in an explanation, they should not force themselves to provide the explanation to the detriment of the speaker's other comments. But paradoxically, a brief explanation can actually save time in the long run. This is the case if a notion is used repeatedly in a speech. Then, the interpreter can explain its meaning the first time it is mentioned and thereafter refer to it in an abbreviated form, thus saving time.

For example, the French are (rightfully) very proud of their high speed trains, and when they say '*the* TGV' [= train à grande vitesse = high-speed train], they mean pretty well by definition *their* high-speed train, the French one. One could interpret a speech about the TGV by saying, each time it is mentioned, 'the French high-speed train'. But you would save time if you slipped in the first time, 'the TGV, that is, the French high speed train', and thereafter just repeated the French initials, which the delegate would then understand.

As in consecutive, this use of explanation must be made to the appropriate audience. One should not insult a gathering of European railway experts by telling them what the TGV is. It should also be done in the most scrupulous, objective and economical way possible, not expressing any personal view of the interpreter.

Anticipation

Even with the precautions mentioned above concerning the moment to begin speaking in simultaneous interpretation, the distance to maintain from the speaker and the need to avoid launching into sentences one cannot finish, it is clear that the interpreter must often begin a sentence without knowing exactly where that sentence is going. To alleviate this difficulty the simultaneous interpreter must learn to anticipate.

First, it is possible to anticipate the broad structure and sometimes the general thrust of a speech. This anticipation can be possible from the context of a meeting. If there is a discussion or a negotiation delegations' positions or arguments will become known, they will return to points they have already made, or react to points made by other participants. A delegate who has expressed severe criticism of a point of view may attenuate their position or compromise, but they will not turn around and suddenly wholeheartedly endorse that point of view. Such anticipation will be enhanced if the interpreter can also bring to bear other cognitive knowledge available to them. If you are interpreting a politician with notoriously liberal views on all things economic, that politician is not going to declare their opposition to deregulation and liberalisation of postal services, for example.

Second, interpreters should learn to recognize speech patterns and rhetorical structures, particularly in the languages they have to interpret from. Those working from English should know that an Englishman or woman who begins with, 'This is an interesting idea/ingenious argument/tempting proposition' and so on is very liable to continue, 'but...'. Interpreters working from German should be aware that a German speech structure is often ternary: 1) Here is my position; 2) This is why this is my position; 3) Let me sum up my position. A French speaker will tend to use the classical thesis-antithesis-synthesis structure. An Italian, contrary to others (such as the French) who may gradually work their way to a conclusion, may well state their conclusion to begin with, and then argue to explain that conclusion. And so on.

One should not exaggerate such national stereotypes, nor their importance, but they can help an interpreter to anticipate. Above all, if the interpreter is given tips by the speaker as to what is coming next, they should use that information. It may seem too obvious to be worthwhile stating, but if a speaker uses, for example, the thesis-antithesis-synthesis approach and presents the thesis then continues, 'but on the other hand...', the interpreter has to be alert to this; they have to anticipate (in their mind, not in their spoken word) the general thrust, if not the detail, of the counter-argument.

Third, interpreters can anticipate specific words or phrases in individual sentences because it is simply so obvious how the sentence is going to end. This is particularly important when working from a source language that has quite different syntax from the target language. To deal with this problem, the interpreter uses reformulation in any case, but there are occasions when waiting for a key word, which would allow the interpreter to formulate their own sentence, would take so long that it is better to anticipate. There are also instances where either technique is possible, but it is just much easier to anticipate.

Non-interpreters with a knowledge of foreign languages often ask interpreters who work from German how they cope, 'because you often have to wait for the verb at the end of the sentence'. This is a classic example of where anticipation can be used. One could just as well ask how two German speakers in conversation with one another cope. Does the one listening have to wait for the verb to be spoken by the other before they suddenly understand? Surely they understand the sentence as it is being spoken.

Thus, for example, the French delegation has presented a document. Various delegations are thanking them for it, and the German delegation says (with German word order), 'We too should like the French delegation for its very useful document to thank'. The interpreter should know practically as soon as the German delegate pronounces the first words that the verb at the end will be *to thank*. There may even be other clues along the way. The German delegate may add the adverb *warmly*: 'We too should like warmly the French delegation...'. This can only confirm the interpreter's intuition.

If the interpreter's intuition tells them a sentence must end in a particular way, even before the words are spoken, then the interpreter can actually anticipate, not just in their mind but in their interpretation, saying the words before the speaker does. This may make formulation easier for them. It can give them a breathing space and extra time to work in for subsequent sentences. Nasty surprises cannot be totally ruled out, but the interpreter who uses anticipation intelligently will find that the advantages accruing from the ninety-nine times they get it right will outweigh the drawbacks of the one time in a hundred that they anticipate wrongly and have to correct their interpretation.

This form of anticipation is a technique that lends itself particularly well to interpreting from Germanic languages (not just German), in particular because of the need to anticipate verbs. But it can be used for all source languages. In all languages interpreters will identify verbs that, in context, necessarily require a particular subject or object (which may come much later in the speaker's sentence), a modal verb that calls for a particular main verb, etc. Particularly useful will be the ability to make the crucial anticipation of a negative concept expressed at the end of a sentence (e.g. 'This is an idea which will please nobody').

We must conclude with a caveat. Anticipation can be a precious tool. Used in conjunction with reformulation it can help improve significantly the interpreter's expression and provide time savings. But its proper use presupposes that the interpreter is always working in context, continues to listen attentively to the speaker, and does not prejudge the issue so much that they end up making their own speech, saying what they feel should be logical, rather than following the speaker.

What if I Make a Clear Mistake?

As mentioned, anticipation can go wrong. What should you do if this happens? The answer to this question applies to all cases where the simultaneous interpreter makes a clear, objective mistake and then realizes what they have done. Such errors can occur for reasons other than a mistake in anticipation. You can mishear a word, not hear a word at all (which can have dramatic consequences if that word is 'not'), misunderstand a word or phrase, misconstrue a speaker's logic, interpret incorrectly a reference by the speaker that was merely implicit in the original, make a slip of the tongue and say incorrectly something that you have understood perfectly, etc.

If a mistake is made there are a number of possible scenarios. First, it is possible for the interpreter to make a mistake on a point that has little or no bearing on the way the meeting proceeds, perhaps an aside by the speaker, and nobody has noticed. The interpreter, out of professional pride, may feel it is desirable to correct themselves and give the right version to their audience. However, I feel that if the error makes no material difference it is a waste of time, both for the interpreter and for their delegates, to make the correction, and the interpreter should just pass it over in silence.

Second, the interpreter might make a mistake on a point that is more signifi-cant, but it then becomes obvious from the behaviour of their audience that they have mentally rectified in any case. Perhaps the interpreter has given a wrong page reference and from context the delegates know what the page is, or the interpreter has said something that is logically inconsistent or technically im-possible and the delegates can work out what the truth must be. In such a case it is not necessary for the interpreter to make a correction for the good order of the meeting. But if they can slip in a correction quickly it is a good idea, as it will improve (or restore) the delegates' confidence in their interpreter and generally establish a better personal relationship between interpreter and audience. It is preferable to make the correction in a matter-of-fact way, with an apology, as if you were merely correcting a slip of the tongue in a normal conversation: 'Sorry, the speaker is referring to page 24, not 42'.

Finally, the interpreter might make a clear material mistake that is impor-tant, and their audience does not realize it. As soon as the interpreter sees this has happened, they must swallow their pride and correct the point as quickly and as clearly as possible. It is totally unethical for an interpreter to try to 'cover up' for a mistake just to avoid the embarrassment of admitting it.

Such scenarios are to be clearly distinguished from those cases where the interpreter has essentially translated correctly but feels they could express them-selves still better, more elegantly, more idiomatically or more exactly. In this latter case the interpreter should not backtrack to correct themselves. Such cor-rections are not only unnecessary, as the only purpose they serve is to satisfy the interpreter's own desire to provide a 'perfect' translation, but they are also inef-ficient, as they will prevent the audience from concentrating on the message they are supposed to be hearing, and the interpreter from concentrating on the speaker's subsequent words.

What if the Speaker Makes a Mistake?

The very first thing to say about speakers' mistakes is that they happen less frequently than interpreters think. It is rare for an interpreter to be in a position where they can judge the content of a speaker's comments and identify mis-takes just on the basis of the knowledge the interpreter brings with them to the meeting. How often has an interpreter sat there, finding the speaker's comments strange, saying to themselves 'This *can't* be true!' only to find that after all it was true? Extreme caution is to be exercised by any interpreter ascribing an error to a speaker.

However, there are occasions when the interpreter can be sure they have spotted a mistake made by a delegate. The delegate may make a slip of the tongue, for example situating a famous event in the wrong century. They may make a reference to something said in the course of a meeting, for example if the Italian delegation has spent five minutes arguing in favour of stricter environmental limits and the German delegation says, 'Italy is in favour of less strict environmental limits'. A delegate might misquote the number of a document. And so on. In this kind of objective situation, where the interpreter is at least ninety-nine percent sure that a mistake has been made, they can react.

As with one's own mistakes, there are a number of possible scenarios. First, it may be that the speaker really has just made a slip of the tongue. The discussion is whether five hundred thousand or five hundred and fifty thousand dollars should be allocated to a project, and one delegate pleads for 'five hundred million' (perhaps having already talked of 'half a million'). This is obviously a slip of the tongue; it would be a waste of time to repeat the speaker's words and then offer a putative correction to the audience. It is better simply to interpret this as 'five hundred thousand'.

Second, the speaker might be saying something quite wrong and the interpreter feels they know what the right version should be, but are not totally sure. For example, a scientist says, 'Given the fire hazard, we need to look for an inert, light gas, such as hydrogen'. The gas in question cannot be hydrogen. Given the context of the meeting, the interpreter deduces it is helium, but cannot be totally sure. The interpreter should therefore interpret the speaker's sentence faithfully, and then add as quickly as possible, '...says the speaker, but I think he means helium'. This shows no disrespect for the speaker and will give the audience all the information they require. At the same time it does not commit the interpreter to the term 'helium'. If the gas turns out to be a third one, the interpreter cannot be blamed for mistranslating and misleading the audience, as they have merely put forward a plausible hypothesis.

Third, the speaker might say something clearly wrong but the interpreter has no clear idea what the correct text would be. Then, the interpreter should proceed as in the second scenario but not give any alternative, thus just adding to the speaker's words, '...says the speaker'. This same technique is to be used if the speaker's mistake is based on a misconception that it is necessary to highlight in order to restore clarity to the meeting. Let's return to the example above, where the Italian delegation argues clearly and at length for stricter environmental limits, and the German delegation says, 'As the Italian delegation wants less strict environmental limits...'. This could be a slip of the tongue. But it could also be that the German delegation has misunderstood, was unattentive, or was out of the room when the Italian delegation was making its comments and is unaware that the Italian position has changed. It might just be, also, that the German delegation wants *still more stringent* limits than Italy, and is being sarcastic! Prudence is therefore necessary on the side of the interpreter, but to avoid a continuation of misunderstanding in the room they should add to the

German delegate's words, '...says the speaker'. This should function as a kind of warning signal for the interpreter's audience, and if the German delegation really has misunderstood, the situation can be straightened out.

Two concluding comments are in order on possible mistakes made by speakers. There is the situation where a delegate, for organizational reasons, is unable to speak their mother tongue and does not fully master the language they use in the meeting. If such a delegate gets tangled up in their comments, saying odd things, contradicting themselves, using double negatives when one negative is sufficient to express their meaning, the interpreter should show sensitivity and express to the best of their ability the ideas they understand the speaker wishes to express. There is no point repeatedly saying 'says the speaker'. If the speaker's message is really unclear, the interpreter may, at the end of a speech, make one overall remark to the effect that they are not totally sure of the speaker's meaning as the speaker has to speak a foreign language.

Generally, again, corrections or expressions of doubt as to whether a speaker has made a mistake should be kept to the strict minimum. Better to intervene in this way too rarely than too often. If such remarks from the interpreter are too frequent this will only irritate their delegates. If, once in a while, a speaker makes a mistake, the interpreter translates it faithfully and correctly and then afterwards the delegates, in bad faith, claim it was the fault of the interpreter who has made a translation error, then that's just too bad. It will not happen too often, and the interpreter should just put up with it phlegmatically.

Avoiding Committing Yourself

When using anticipation the interpreter will note all the signs given by a speaker as to what will come next, and make use of those signs. However, they will not reveal to their audience that they have received these signs: they will not announce to the audience what should follow.

This may seem a strange comment in the light of what was said above about consecutive. In consecutive you should definitely interpret such useful structuring elements as, 'I should like to make three comments on this proposal', and then proceed to enumerate the three points. We even said that if the speaker does not provide such elements, and if the structures helps to improve the audience's understanding, the interpreter may add them of their own accord. Why then should the simultaneous interpreter go to the other extreme?

The answer, quite simply, is that one can never trust a speaker to provide what they have announced in advance. In consecutive, you have heard the whole speech and can interpret accordingly. If the speaker announced three points and then enunciated only two, or four, the consecutive interpreter can choose to skip the announcement, or correct it to bring it into line with reality. But in simultaneous, no such possibility exists. Again, one could argue that if the speaker gets it wrong, that's their problem, and it is not up to the interpreter to cover for them. But if one adopts a client-oriented approach, saying that the interpreter will convey the speaker's message with greatest faithfulness to the original but also greatest clarity and ease of comfort for the listener, then there is no point sending your audience signals that will either have to be countermanded or will actually contradict what follows.

It must also be admitted that a speaker may announce, say, a certain number of points and respect that structure, but it is then the interpreter who fails in simultaneous to pick out all of the elements to match that structure. However, it is more often the speaker, not the interpreter, who is the weak link in the chain and who causes difficulties.

Thus, if a speaker announces, 'I should like to make three comments on this proposal', the interpreter should note the fact but not announce it to their audience, either saying nothing at all, or something rather vaguer, such as, 'I should like to make some comments on this proposal'.

The same thing applies, for example, to a speaker who announces a joke. Even in normal conversation it is dangerous to announce a joke. The listeners' expectations are raised, and if the joke is only mediocre, the whole thing is liable to fall flat. In interpretation, things are much worse. To make a comic effect, the interpreter is not dependent only on themselves but also on the speaker, who may be quite unfunny. And even if the speaker is funny in the source language, jokes are notoriously difficult to translate; the joke may depend on an untranslatable pun, or may just not seem funny to someone of a different language and culture from the speaker. Thus a joke should not be announced. If it is really funny, and everyone laughs, then the interpreter need say no more. If the humour is not necessarily conveyed, and the interpreter is afraid that a humorous remark might be taken too seriously, or even offend somebody because of a misunderstanding, then the interpreter should provide a word of explanation. They can say something like, 'But that is not a comment to be taken seriously', or 'But I'm only joking'.

As a parenthesis here, we might mention some rules for dealing with jokes in simultaneous. If the joke is translatable, then the interpreter should obviously do their best to render it. As the speaker will be hoping for comic effect and some response from their audience, and as those who listen to the speaker directly will react as soon as the speaker has told their joke, this is a case where the interpreter should try to be very close in time to the speaker, so that the audience reaction is simultaneous, or nearly, throughout the room.

If the joke is not translatable, for example if it is a pun, the interpreter can try providing some other light, humorous treatment of the text, to achieve a similar result. If that is not possible – and I admit it is extremely difficult to do off the cuff – then the interpreter must fall back on informing their audience that the speaker is making an untranslatable joke or pun. If they have time, they can even explain the essence of the joke. Some interpreters, when they see that a speaker is determined to raise a laugh, use the tactic of saying something like, 'The speaker is telling an untranslatable joke now, which he thinks is very funny, and will expect everyone to laugh. To oblige him and the interpreters, would you be so kind as to laugh... *now!*' This trick, if not overused, can usually have sufficient comic effect on its own to make the audience laugh at just the right moment, and everyone can feel satisfied.

To return to the topic of not committing oneself, literary allusions ('as it says in the Bible...', 'in the words of Shakespeare...', etc.), historical quotations ('let me say in the words of Sir Winston Churchill...') and all other such clauses with annunciatory effect are to be shunned, as you can never be sure you will be able to render correctly the passage that has been announced. It is far better to concentrate on interpreting the passage as well as you can. Later, if appropriate, the interpreter can add, 'as Shakespeare wrote', or conceivably, if they feel their interpretation is not up to the high literary standard of the original, something like 'to paraphrase Shakespeare'.

In the case of literary and historical quotations, this caution is particularly important if the original quotation was written or said in the interpreter's target language but the speaker in the meeting is now quoting it in a different language. For example, if an English speaker says, 'I feel I could say, in the words of Goethe...' and a German interpreter has to interpret. A German interpreter can get away with paraphrasing Shakespeare or Dante, but the German delegate will expect to hear the right quotation from Goethe and much of the speaker's effect will be lost (and the German delegate disappointed) if the interpreter misquotes. The interpreter's own translation of the English speaker's version of Goethe, and then the words, 'to paraphrase Goethe' is a much safer bet.

Metaphors and Sayings

The same rule should be used for not announcing metaphors and sayings when a speaker tells their audience that they are about to use one. On the one hand there is the risk that the interpreter will not understand the saying. If the speaker says something like, 'As we say in Bohemia, that would be turning the billy-goat into a gardener', the interpreter cannot do very much with this (if they do not know the exact saying). If they have announced the saying, they are obliged to come up with something.

On the other hand, the interpreter may understand the saying or metaphor but then find that exactly the same thing exists in the target language. If the interpreter says, 'As we say in western Moravia...', then comes out with a really typical English saying such as 'Don't count your chickens before they're hatched', the English-speaking delegates listening to the interpretation are going to find the English interpreter extremely strange.

The same argument applies even if the saying in the source language does not exist word-for-word in the target language but has an exact equivalent in meaning. 'Don't count your chickens...' in French is literally, 'One mustn't sell the bearskin before killing the bear'. If a French-speaking delegate says this and the target language is English, the interpreter should not translate it literally and explain 'as the saying goes in French'. The delegates are not in the meeting to appreciate the curiosities of foreign languages; the interpreter should give the English equivalent of the French saying, with no qualification.

Thus, sayings and metaphors should not be announced. They should be interpreted into the corresponding form in the target language, where possible, without further explanation. If the meaning of the saying is clear to the interpreter but the saying does not have an equivalent in the target language, the interpreter should express the sense to the best of their ability without being put off by the form used by the speaker. If the interpreter cannot even understand the meaning of the saying, they should ask themselves whether it is important enough for them to do something about. It is conceivable that they could just miss it out. If, however, they do not understand and the saying is important – for example it is used to express the speaker's conclusion at the end of a complicated line of argument and is thus crucial to understanding the speaker's position – the interpreter can only translate the saying as literally as possible and announce to their audience that this is, for example, a traditional Moravian saying. The hope is that the audience will either work out from the interpreter's translation what is meant, or, if they cannot understand, will ask for a clarification from the speaker.

Another important rule is that interpreters should avoid creating their own metaphors and images in a meeting. Let's say one delegate says in language A, 'The current proposal is imbalanced. It really needs to cover all four areas, but only three are covered'. An interpreter has a 'brainwave' and the notion of 'three out of four' conjures up the image for them of a chair with one leg missing, having only three to stand upon. They interpret into language B: 'The current proposal is imbalanced. It's like a chair that should have four legs but only has three, as only three of the four areas have been covered'. That interpreter's delegate feels this is an useful image and uses it in their own reply. The interpreter working into language A, who has heard no mention of a chair, will be mystified. If, however, the interpreter working into A manages to interpret it correctly, it will then be the turn of their delegates to be totally confused.

The problem is bad enough if the meeting is taking place in only two languages. But if something similar happens in a meeting with, say, ten languages, there will be havoc. The bald statement is made by a delegate in language A. It is interpreted as an image about a chair into B, but not into the eight other languages. Delegate B re-uses the image. What now? There may be interpreters who realize this is the invention of a colleague and choose to ignore it. Others may feel it is safer to follow the speaker. Soon you are in a situation where half the room is not using the metaphor while the other half is. Further, as delegates are wont to do, those that use the metaphor start modifying it: 'No,' says one of them, 'if we add another point, it will be a five-legged stool'. The mind boggles at the potential for misunderstanding.

Therefore, while it is a good thing for an interpreter to have a rich vocabulary and a wide range of expressions at their disposal, and while it can be useful for some interpreters to visualize vividly the speeches they hear, in order to enhance their understanding, such artificial creation of images for the audience's consumption is to be avoided.

Using 'Pat Phrases'

'Pat', in this sense, according to the Oxford English Dictionary, means 'known thoroughly and ready for any occasion'. There are many formulations that occur frequently in international meetings. Any given interpreter may also find that in their own professional life, depending on their employer or clients, certain turns of phrase crop up particularly often, not to say practically all the time. For such circumstances all interpreters should have a battery of pat phrases that they can use without having to make any intellectual effort. This will help them economize their energies, allowing them to concentrate more on genuinely problematic things. It will also provide them with yet one more technique for saving time, as such pat phrases can be produced extremely quickly.

What kind of circumstance can these phrases be prepared for? For example, delegates often say they 'agree' or 'disagree', that they 'support', 'endorse', 'back' ideas; that they 'call into question', 'wonder about', 'have doubts about' them; that they 'understand' or 'don't understand', as the case may be, that they have 'grasped' an idea, 'require clarification', 'want something specified'. If an interpreter is involved in work that involves a lot of discussion about documents and drafting, they should have turns of phrase for deleting and adding, for strengthening or attenuating a text; all technical editing terms should be known by heart – paragraphs, sub-paragraphs, points, indents, etc.; and all typical drafting jargon should become second nature – 'in particular', 'inter alia', 'as appropriate', and so on. Those dealing with regulatory texts should be aware of how they function and have the relevant turns of phrase available: waivers, exceptions, exemptions, opt-outs, time limits, expiry dates, field of competence, scope, etc.

The list of examples is endless, and it is up to each interpreter to see where such preparation is necessary and build up the appropriate body of pat phrases. I insist that this is not just a case of knowing *vocabulary* which is relevant to subject areas or the type of work that an interpreter typically does. It is a question of having the right *formulations* ready to hand.

For example, let's assume a delegate says (word-for-word) in the source language: 'The time period for this regulation runs until the end of the year, and we need a decision on its prolongation before the year is over if we are not to be faced with a legal vacuum.'

The interpreter should, as far as possible, have ready solutions for every element in such a sentence. The first clause can become, in English, 'The regulation expires at the end of the year'. The notion of expiry must come immediately to the interpreter. Similarly, they should know (in this hypothetical case, and assuming that that is the jargon used) that the regulation is 'extended' in time, and be able to say, 'We must, therefore, decide on its extension by then'. Even a phrase as innocent as 'by then', or 'by the end of the year', is the kind of thing that can cause unnecessary waste of time and effort for an interpreter. If it does not fit into their repertory of pat phrases interpreters may find themselves, from certain source languages, saying something as complicated (and superfluous) as 'between now and the end of the year'. Moreover, they will have made a deliberate, and again unnecessary, mental effort to decide how they wish to express the idea.

Intonation, Stress and Pauses

When people communicate they express what they want to say not just through the words they use but also by intonation, by stressing certain words, and by pauses between words. A simultaneous interpreter should be no exception to this rule (cf. 're-expression' in the chapter on consecutive).

Unfortunately, simultaneous interpreters are subject to a number of constraints and temptations that may prevent them from using intonation, stress and pauses correctly. The first problem is that the simultaneous interpreter is in a sound-proof booth, behind double-glazing, sometimes a long way from their delegates (for example in large conference rooms where the booths are installed high up like a film projectionist's room in a cinema). All of this can lead to the interpreter feeling cut off from the proceedings and thus rather indifferent to them. The upshot of this is that the interpreter is liable to interpret like an automaton, without using the potential of their voice to enhance meaning. There are no technical means for overcoming this problem. The only thing we can do is encourage interpreters to take an active interest in their meetings, to try to feel involved, in the ways we mentioned at the very beginning of this chapter.

Second, there is the risk that interpreters may feel under pressure to keep up a continuous flow of sound in the booth. They are worried that if they do not keep talking, their delegates will become impatient and lose confidence in the interpreter because they are frightened they are missing something. Sadly, there are some delegates who encourage interpreters in this belief, who *do* turn round and frown or make gestures indicating they feel their headphones are no longer working if they do not hear something for a few seconds. Interpreters should have the courage to stand up to such pressure from delegates and ignore their reactions. On the contrary, the interpreter should know that appropriate pauses do add to the meaning of a speech and give them the time to gather their thoughts in order to provide a better interpretation.

A third error not to fall into is an overreaction to being under pressure, which manifests itself by an exaggerated attempt to sound cool and calm. This can lead interpreters to sound totally bored, if not supercilious (which is very irritating for the audience), and to provide a monotonous interpretation that, having no relief, will probably fail to communicate as much as it should, having a soporific effect on the delegates.

Fourth, some go to the other extreme, providing too much stress, emphasizing words that do not deserve it, and generally hamming it up. This risk is greater if the text is uninteresting, not to say vacuous, and the interpreter feels obliged to compensate for the lack of real content by livening up the presentation. Sadly, this will only highlight the actual emptiness of the text and make the interpreters poor public speakers. One arrives at a presentation such as the following, where the interpreter stresses all of the words we have put in italics: 'What we *really* want to do is *come forward* with some *concrete*, *practical* proposals in the *social* sphere, so that the *social* as well as the *economic* aspects are addressed....'

The fifth difficulty is of a more technical nature, in that it is related to the fact that the simultaneous interpreter does not know how a speaker is going to proceed. The interpreter's intonation may indicate that they are always in a state of expectation, waiting for what comes next. When you are in an expectant, questioning frame of mind, your voice tends to go up at the end of a sentence. In many languages a rising intonation at the end of a phrase indicates either a question or surprise, or that one has not finished a sentence and another clause is to follow. If the interpreter systematically goes up at the end of their sentences it becomes very difficult for their audience to listen and understand where sentences begin and end, or to distinguish what is affirmative and what is interrogative.

The answer to this difficulty lies in having the right general approach to speaking in simultaneous, as described above. When the interpreter begins a sentence, they should be able to finish it, even if they do not know exactly *how* they will finish it. As the speaker's sentence proceeds, it should become clear to the interpreter how to finish their own (interpreted) sentence. And once the interpreter knows how they can finish their sentence they must make a conscious decision to do so, and to signal the end clearly to their audience by a falling intonation. If the interpreter does not wish to finish a sentence, adding another main clause or a subordinate or relative clause, then they should likewise signal to their audience that the sentence is continuing by using the right intonation.

Provided the interpreter is in control of their own output in this way, they should be able to use intonation as suggested in the chapter on consecutive. They should not make artificial pauses in the middle of a sentence because they are thinking of what to say next or are waiting for extra input from the speaker. Of course, if a speaker suddenly pauses for a long time because they themselves have lost the thread or are wondering how to continue, there is nothing the simultaneous interpreter can do.

Sentences should be clearly separated by the appropriate intonation and, if necessary, a brief pause. Sentences should not be strung out endlessly with 'and... and... and...'. Paragraphs and sections in a speech should be clearly denoted by slightly longer pauses in the interpretation. Insofar as an interpreter uses rhetorical devices – including rhetorical questions – or is expressing surprise, emotion, etc., they should accompany the words with the right intonation.

Numbers

Numbers can be very difficult for simultaneous interpreters and can be absolutely crucial pieces of information where no error is permissible. In particular, numbers have an objective meaning and are in no way open to linguistic interpretation. For these reasons, it is important to work out a tactic for coping with them.

First, one must realize that numbers, as used in meetings, are much more complex than they at first seem. When an interpreter is confronted with a number, they have to deal not just with the bare arithmetical value but with as many as five elements. The first element is the arithmetic value. The second element is part of that arithmetic value, but should be identified as a specific element by the interpreter, namely the order of magnitude. It is important to give the right order of magnitude in interpretation. If you are talking about the temperature in thermonuclear fusion and talk of thousands of degrees, rather than millions, this will be no use to the audience. Even if the other elements in the number quoted are correct, the audience will not be able to make any sense at all of the number, or if they can will probably not trust the interpreter anyway and will ask the speaker for a clarification. The third element is the unit. It can make all the difference in the world if prices are quoted in dollars but are then interpreted as deutschmarks, pounds sterling or euros, or if in textile negotiations one party gives figures that relate to 'thousand pieces' and these are interpreted as tons. The fourth element is what the numbers refer to. Is it cane sugar or beet sugar, raw sugar or refined sugar? And the fifth element is the relative value of a number. Is it being quoted in isolation as a fixed value, or is it being quoted as an increase or a decrease, and if so in relation to what, and by how much or in what proportion? In dealing with this last point the interpreter must be very vigilant, since relative values can sometimes be stated, through no fault of the speaker, in a very ambiguous way. For example, it is possible to say in some languages, 'The spot price has increased by/from $2.1 to $252.3 per ton', where 'by' and 'from' can be expressed by the same word. In the example given, it is obvious which of the two it must be, given the figures: this shows the importance of working from context and identifying the order of magnitude, so as to avoid talking nonsense. Even so, there will be occasions when it is much less clear what is meant. The first thing, then, is to be aware of these five elements and to deal with as many of them as are present in the original.

When it comes to dealing with a number as an arithmetical value, an interpreter will be able to deal with one number easily, even retaining a fairly complex number in their short-term memory for a number of seconds as they interpret other elements in the sentence. However, once two or more numbers are quoted, the interpreter will need some assistance other than pure memory. The second technique, therefore, is that, if at all possible, the interpreter should unload their memory and say numbers as soon as possible after the speaker has said them. This means modulating the distance they keep from the speaker. Just as in consecutive you note numbers immediately, even if that means leaving some other element in your notes and coming back to it later, so in simultaneous the interpreter should be as close as possible to the speaker in order to repeat numbers immediately. This can cause difficulties if in preceding sentences the interpreter was some distance behind the speaker for all of the reasons described above. Therefore, if the interpreter senses that numbers are going to be given, they should accelerate their own speech so as to catch up with the speaker. If a speaker announces numbers with a phrase such as 'Let me provide you with some statistics', the interpreter may do well to skip that sentence altogether, as it will make it easier for them to catch up totally on the speaker. If the interpreter cannot catch up with the speaker, they must finish the sentence preceding the numbers as quickly as possible and then move on to the sentence including the numbers *by saying the numbers first*. This is another application of reformulation as discussed above. If the speaker says, 'Imports of jeans from China have increased by 9.3%, from the Philippines by 6.5%...', the interpreter can interpret '9.3% is the increase in jeans imports from China, 6.5% from the Philippines...', so as to say the numbers instantaneously.

If the numbers are coming thick and fast, however, this technique alone will probably not solve all of the interpreter's problems. A further thing you can do is note down the numbers as they hear them. This means unburdening your memory immediately so you can concentrate on interpreting the rest of the sentence, fitting the numbers in as appropriate. A further advantage in writing down numbers is that it should reduce the risk of misinterpretation for difficult numbers and make fast interpretation easier. If someone hears a number, in whatever language, they can usually write it down in Arabic numerals without any effort.

The same goes for the interpreter: when hearing a number they do not need to think in terms of its translation into another language. Then, if the number is written down, by looking at the Arabic numerals the interpreter should be able to read off, with no effort, the number in the target language. The interpreter will thus have transposed a number from one language to another without having mentally gone through a translation process.

For example, for numbers between twenty and one hundred there are some languages that express them 'twenty-two, twenty-three', etc. and other languages that express them 'two-and-twenty, three-and-twenty', etc. Between such languages it is only too easy to misinterpret, for example, 'forty-eight [eight-and-forty]' as 'eighty-four'. If, however, you write down '48' on hearing it, then you should have no difficulty in saying it correctly. The interpreter alert to the danger can even make things safer by writing down the '8' first and then the '4' afterwards, to the left of the first digit, thus writing from right to left but arriving at the right number.

Other than this, writing down numbers can be helpful for coping with a whole range of 'complicated' numbers in various languages. There are the famous examples in French of the numbers in the 70s – 'sixty-ten to sixty nineteen' – and the 80s and 90s – 'four-score to four-score-nineteen'. Converting these through numerals, rather than translating them, can be quicker and easier. Not to mention Danish numbers, particularly ordinal numbers, between fifty and one hundred. Actually *translating* 'five-and-half-three-score-th' into 'fifty-fifth' may not come so easily, but if the interpreter understands the number and writes down '55th', then there should be no real problem.

Writing down numbers is an area where there can, and should, be real team work in the booth. A colleague who shares a source language with an interpreter who is interpreting should write down the numbers for their colleague. They can concentrate exclusively on the numbers. They need not, indeed should not, bother about other elements in the speech. We say 'should not', as they should write down *solely* the relevant numbers, possibly with the units. If they try to write down more they are likely just to confuse their colleague. The whole point is to ease the burden of dealing with the numbers for the interpreter who is 'on mike', such that they can get on and deal with all the other elements in the original. It goes without saying that if you write down numbers for a colleague you should make sure they are very readable, preferably writing extremely large.

There are occasions when numbers have to be interpreted absolutely accurately, with every digit correct. An example would be customs tariff codes, where the ninth and tenth digits can be crucial, as they determine a tariff classification. However, there are also occasions where it is possible to be more approximate. Let's assume that a speaker says, 'The tariff quota is 300 tons, and use up to 19th August has been 295.6 tons, so the quota has been almost totally exhausted, with four months of the year to run'. Here the key element expressed by the second number is that the use is very nearly 300 tons. If the interpreter is not totally sure of the detail of the second figure, they could interpret by making an intelligent approximation, saying, '...and use up to 19th August is two hundred and ninety-odd tons, so...'. Of course, it is better not to make such approximations, but interpreters should be aware of when an approximation is possible, and be able to fall back on it if necessary. Examples here would be situations were there is a sequence of numbers where it is well nigh impossible to interpret them all, or where there are other very difficult elements in a speech that the interpreter needs to be able to concentrate upon.

Finally, interpreters can choose to express numbers in the way they find most convenient. For example, a speaker may say, 'We have allocated six million five hundred and forty-three thousand dollars to the project'. The way this is expressed in different languages will of course depend on certain rules that cannot be infringed. But there might also be options open to the interpreter. One interpreter into English could choose to express this number exactly as in the original. But another may find it easier and quicker to say 'six point five four three million dollars'. This is very much a question of personal taste and convenience, but even when interpreting numbers, interpreters should be on the look-out for formulations that make life easier for them and save time without sacrificing information.

'Retour'

If a professional conference interpreter works into a language other than their mother tongue and is thus engaged in 'retour' interpreting, they should be able to interpret accurately, clearly and with correct grammar. As mentioned in the introductory chapter, an interpreter may choose to limit their retour to working from their mother tongue. Even so, the difficulties in retour can be different from those experienced when working into your mother tongue.

When listening to a foreign language and interpreting it into your mother tongue, the main linguistic and intellectual problem you will have will be understanding the ideas expressed in the original. As a general rule, the interpreter should have the active linguistic means in their mother tongue to cope with re-expressing those ideas once they have been understood. On the other hand, in retour the interpreter may sometimes find they have more difficulty in finding the best way to convey the ideas they have understood. This is particularly the case when the retour is from the mother tongue. The interpreter understands their mother tongue so intimately and intuitively that it is easy to have the feeling that they are not doing justice to the original, that there are nuances not being conveyed. If the interpreter develops such a feeling, they can find the experience very frustrating.

In retour, then, a certain number of things have to be borne in mind. First, the interpreter should accept that there are certain nuances, shades of meaning or stylistic niceties that they will not be able to express, particularly from their mother tongue. They must remember that the interpreter is there to make communication possible. They must thus concentrate on conveying the speakers' ideas, and not fall into the trap of trying to provide a perfectionist translation, which in any case is impossible.

Imagine, for example, an interpreter is doing a retour from English, and their speaker says:

> It is a rather wry irony of fate that the country which gave the world *The General Theory of Employment, Interest and Money* should now be held up by the monetarist groupies of the Chicago School as a model for neoliberal practice.

The sentence begins with a typically English turn of phrase that is difficult to render exactly in many other languages, particularly the notoriously difficult notion 'wry'. The interpreter may have to give up on trying to render every nuance of this and begin with [literally] 'It is an irony of history that...' Then, perhaps the interpreter does not know the exact title of *The General Theory* in their retour language and would prefer to avoid misquoting. They could continue, 'the country which gave the world Keynes'. This is a handy shortcut, and conveys the idea just as well. Third, the connotations of 'groupies' are difficult to convey if one does not have to hand the exact same word in the target language (as this is modern jargon, it is possible that no such word actually exists in the target language). The interpreter might have to fall back on calling them simply 'fans', 'supporters', 'partisans', or something like that, even though the rather deprecating tone of 'groupies' is thereby lost. And so on. Interpreting like this, some of the flavour of the original may be lost, which is regrettable, but the interpreter will have succeeded in their main task of making communication possible.

Second, the interpreter doing a retour should be modest in the style they adopt. As is often advised for sportsmen and women, they must 'play within themselves'. That is, they should not try to do things that are really beyond them stylistically, using a very literary style, or a lot of images, metaphors and similes, cultural references, etc. If the interpreter is confident and in control of the situation they can of course use the stylistic effects they master. But they must not overreach themselves. In particular, the interpreter must be aware of what linguistic register they should be using. You do not speak in the same way if you are an ambassador addressing a diplomatic conference, a scientist in a small technical working party, or a trades unionist discussing strategy with colleagues. This is something that applies to all interpreters, not just in the case of a retour. But it is all the more important for the interpreter doing a retour. They must on the one hand avoid being over-pompous; and on the other, they must avoid being too familiar. There are few things more excruciating than listening to a foreigner speaking one's language and striking the wrong tone by trying to use a colloquial style when this is quite inappropriate.

It is difficult to provide any advice on how to strike the right linguistic register, except to say that interpreters should be aware of two things. The first is that they must be aware of what kind of meeting they are in. The second is that they should be aware that the problem exists, and of the discrepancies between the use of linguistic register in their mother tongue and in their retour language. For example, in English one can often use a simple, rather familiar mode of expression that in certain formal circumstances would be unthinkable in French. The French-language interpreter doing a retour into English should know this and be able to exploit it, as a casual mode of expression can be rather easier to produce than a more formal one. The English-language interpreter doing a retour into French, on the other hand, must make an effort to respect the stiffer, more formal mode used in French.

Third, retour interpreters should make life as easy as possible for themselves by avoiding highly complex grammatical forms. In other words, in retour you should make maximum use of all the techniques for dealing with simultaneous described in this section. In retour, the linguistic difficulties of expression will be marginally greater than when working into the mother tongue. This added difficulty must be compensated for by pure interpreting technique. In particular, the salami technique should be used to a maximum. The point of the salami technique is to provide the interpreter with short, simple, self-contained sentences where they are less likely to make grammatical mistakes, to forget how they began a sentence, or otherwise to have difficulties of expression. It is obviously a technique that is most pertinent to a situation where the interpreter's difficulties may lie rather more on the expression side than on the understanding side, namely retour. Similarly, in retour you should have the appropriate stock of 'pat phrases' available, to avoid having to make the extra effort of thinking, quite unnecessarily, about turns of phrase that come up repeatedly.

Relay

When an interpreter serves as a relay they are working under special circumstances that have to be taken into account. Not only are they working for an audience directly but their interpretation also has to serve as a source text for one or more colleagues. Some interpreters argue that an interpreter should not change their working method when they are being taken on relay. Their interpretation should in any case be good enough to serve as a source text; colleagues should know their passive languages well enough to cope with anything their relay can throw at them.

That argument would be valid in an ideal world, but I feel a more pragmatic approach is needed to working as relay. First, the relay should give absolute priority to clarity in their interpretation. The content the relay provides for colleagues must be absolutely limpid. An interpreter may be able to interpret quite satisfactorily for their delegates by leaving things implicit, or using a casual, even conversational style that delegates can understand instinctively. But when they are working for colleagues too they must leave no shadow of doubt as to what is meant. Then, clarity is to be provided not just in the content, but also in the form. 'Form' here means the grammatical form, but it also means the relay should articulate particularly clearly, to make sure colleagues can distinguish every syllable they say.

Second, the relay should be closer in time to the original than would other modes of simultaneous. There is a natural time-lag in simultaneous interpreting, and this is necessarily magnified if there are interpreters working on relay. To enable colleagues to be able to finish as closely in time as possible to the speaker, the relay should make sure their time-lag is kept to a minimum, and above all that they are capable of finishing practically simultaneously with the speaker.

Third, you should bear in mind the psychology of the colleagues on relay. To begin with, as is the case for your own delegates, it is necessary to say something almost as soon as you know you are being taken on relay, be it only 'Thank you, Chairman', in order to reassure colleagues and let them know you are there. Thereafter, you should interpret in a calm, smooth way so as to inspire confidence in the colleagues on relay.

Fourth, the relay should remember that the colleagues listening to them may have an imperfect knowledge of the relay language, particularly as far as idiomatic usage and specific cultural references are concerned. The relay, without slipping into an over-simplistic style, should therefore avoid a style that is either abstruse or highly idiomatic. For example, an English-language relay would be well-advised not to interpret along the lines: 'If we add a further demand, not only will our whole negotiating position be thrown out of kilter but we risk being hoist with our own petard'.

Incidentally, this last point is a consideration to be borne in mind generally when working for an audience that is partly or wholly composed of people not listening to their mother tongue. It is a problem that will affect different languages differently. It will be extremely rare for, say, non-Hungarians to listen to a Hungarian interpretation. But at the other end of the scale it will happen very frequently for English-language interpreters, quite often for French-language ones, and it could easily happen to German-language interpreters. If an interpreter is aware that they have a non-mother-tongue audience, they should adapt their style accordingly.

Lastly on relay, one technical point has to be taken into consideration. The relay must make it clear to their colleagues when the language of the original changes. This could involve a change in speaker. Through the relay this may be difficult to identify just from the relay's tone of voice or the content. The relay should therefore announce over the microphone 'the French delegation', or whoever the new speaker is, so that the colleagues know they no longer need be on relay.

But also, a speaker may change languages in the middle of their comments. This is particularly likely if a document that is not available in all of the languages spoken at a meeting is under discussion. Let's say the document is available in English only. The Dutch delegate begins to make certain comments in Dutch. The French interpreters can interpret from Dutch, the Italians cannot. The Italians therefore take the French colleague on relay. Now the Dutch delegate starts quoting in English. The French interpreter should now warn 'in English', such that the Italian colleague, if they desire, can interpret directly from the English spoken by the Dutch delegate. The Italians are all the more likely to want to do this if they have a copy of the text in question in the booth and can refer directly back to it.

There is another circumstance in which it would be even more important for the French interpreter to announce the speaker's change of language. Let's assume the scenario is the same as immediately above, except that the interpreter taking relay from the French booth is in the English booth. When the Dutch delegate starts quoting directly in English, it is important for the English booth to switch off their microphone so that their delegates can listen directly to the English. Otherwise, there will be the absurd situation where the English-speaking delegates will be listening to a translation of a translation of a speech which they could listen to directly. Not only can such a situation be absurd, it can also be very embarrassing. If the English-speaking delegates know the text is in English and that other delegates are liable to quote from it directly, then they may keep one ear on the original. When the Dutch delegate quotes, the English-speaking delegate may hear the original in English and get from the interpreter a version, also in English, but which may be slightly modified. This could hardly inspire the English-speaking delegate to have confidence in their interpreters. A proper warning from the French relay (in this example) could help avoid any such problem.

Concluding Remarks on Simultaneous Technique

Having looked at the range of techniques that can be applied to simultaneous, it is probably useful to identify a common thread running through them all.

The reader might be struck by the number of techniques that involve omitting elements of the original one way or the other. Here we must differentiate between two different forms of omission. There are cases when the interpreter is unfortunately not in a position to provide a totally complete and accurate interpretation. That is regrettable, but it is better to be realistic and recognize there will be such occasions, even in the life of an experienced and competent interpreter. In those circumstances the interpreter omits in order to preserve as much of the essential message as possible. They make an intelligent sacrifice of those parts they think can be omitted at least cost to their audience's understanding, in order to make sure that those elements they do interpret are rendered as clearly and accurately as possible.

On the other hand, there are cases of omission where the interpreter could provide a fuller interpretation but quite deliberately omits with a view to economy of expression, ease of listening for the audience, and maximum communication between speaker and audience.

We hope the reader will therefore not be shocked by the omissions implied in simultaneous technique. In both scenarios – omission under duress and omission from choice (editing) – the objective is the same, namely the best possible communication between participants in a meeting, *given the raw input in the form of the speeches to be interpreted.* The aim of course remains the same for those numerous techniques that do not imply omission. In those, too, the reader will recognize our concern that the interpreter should achieve maximum economy of expression while respecting the sense of the original, both for the interpreter's own convenience and for the convenience of the audience.

The first main thread is thus that the simultaneous interpreter must be prepared to diverge in form, and sometimes in literal content, from the letter of the original, in order to achieve the objectives of a good simultaneous interpretation.

A second common element is that the interpreter has to adapt not just to their speaker but also to the general context of the meeting and to their audience. In other words, interpretation must be audience-specific and situation-specific. This brings us back to the point of departure for all discussion of interpretation. Interpretation is not a solipsistic translation exercise, but a practical job of communication. The interpreter must, above all, be at the service of their client.

Exercises

Getting going on simultaneous

As mentioned above, the two specific difficulties of simultaneous interpreting are acoustic problems and intellectual problems. Rightly or wrongly, we believe there is little that can be done to help students with the acoustic problem except showing them the equipment and giving them practical advice on how to use it. Beyond that, dealing with the acoustic problem is essentially a matter of practice. We thus suggest below a sequenced set of exercises to help students begin simultaneous by trying to deal with what we have dubbed the 'intellectual difficulty'. Initially, the problem of not knowing what comes next is to a large extent eliminated, and only gradually are students brought to deal with speeches that come as a complete surprise to them (cf. in this regard the approach outlined in Dejean Le Féal 1997).

(a)   A student does a speech in consecutive. They are then invited to do the same speech in simultaneous. However, they are requested not to take into the booth the notes taken for consecutive.

(b)   A student listens to a speech, taking notes as if to do a consecutive. However, when the original speech ends they are then invited to go into the booth, without their notes, and do the same speech in simultaneous.

(c)   A student listens to a speech without taking notes and is then invited to go into the booth to do the same speech in simultaneous.

(d)   A student listens to a five-minute speech without taking notes, is invited into the booth, but then the speaker makes a speech which begins like the one the student has heard and continues, on the same topic and with similar vocabulary, for a total of eight to ten minutes.

(e)   The speaker announces their topic and gives a brief summary of the speech. The students may then go into the booth and are asked to do that speech in simultaneous.

(f)   The speaker announces the topic and for a few minutes all those in the class – trainer(s) and students – brainstorm around the topic, mentioning terminology in both the source language and pertinent target languages, and mentioning concepts, lines of argument, ideas that may be developed, etc. The trainer in charge of the class and the speaker (if they are not the same person) should make sure the brainstorming is channelled usefully. The students are then invited to go into the booth to do the speech in simultaneous.

(g)   The speaker announces the topic of the speech and gives no further information: the students then go into the booth to do the speech in simultaneous.

Notes:
1)   Speeches at the beginning of simultaneous training should obviously be fairly easy.
2)   The suggestions made above do not all have to be followed in the given sequence. We of course recommend that they be used flexibly. One or more of the phases can be skipped, depending on the students' needs and the trainers' preferences. Certain exercises may be used in a slightly different order – e.g. (e) and (f) can easily be swapped – provided the general progression toward doing an 'unknown' simultaneous is respected.
3)   When students begin simultaneous their trainers should stress the importance of correctness of interpretation, both in terms of content and form.

Students should get into the good habit of interpreting faithfully and expressing themselves grammatically and in complete sentences even if they miss out quite a lot of information. They must not fall into the bad habit of trying to get everything in and then just parroting mindlessly or talking gobbledegook in the booth. Provided the basic technique of the student is correct they should find it possible over time to build up the quantity of information they manage to interpret. At the beginning, quality comes before quantity.

5. The Pleasure of Interpreting

When interpreters discuss their work with non-interpreters, there are usually two typical reactions from the latter. Some are filled with wonderment, asking how the interpreter does it, finding something almost magical about the ability of simultaneous interpreters to talk and listen at the same time. The other reaction, however, is more sanguine, as non-interpreters ask interpreters whether their job is not too much of a routine or whether they are not frustrated at 'just repeating' what other people say.

The first objection, that of routine, is easy to refute, as should be clear now for the reader. The interpreter is faced with meetings of all kinds, delegates of all kinds, subjects of all kinds. Even when meetings are broadly similar, the challenge to the interpreter can vary considerably: the specific interpreting problems raised by the same delegates in the second meeting of a committee can be quite different from those raised in the first meeting, even if they are talking about the same subject. This is because each speaker will have their own intellectual approach, their own way of expressing themselves. Practically every sentence can bear within it its own intellectual or linguistic puzzle that it is up to the interpreter to resolve.

The answer to the second objection is rather less easy to explain to the non-interpreter. They may well be right: 'just repeating' what someone else says would indeed be boring and frustrating. What they must be brought to see, however, is that their basic assumption about the nature of interpreting is wrong: the interpreter is not 'just repeating'. The key to this lies in everything we have said, both for consecutive and simultaneous, about re-expression and reformulation. The interpreter processes the information they receive from the speaker and creates from it their own line of discourse. In this sense, the work of an interpreter is truly creative.

To approach the question more positively, what are the pleasures of interpreting? Essentially, the pleasure is twofold: social and intellectual.

The social pleasure is that of establishing communication. Communication between people is one of the greatest riches that humankind has. And when there are people who wish to communicate but are prevented from doing so because of linguistic and cultural barriers, it is a privilege for an interpreter to be able to help overcome those barriers. This is true however 'ordinary' or 'unimportant' a meeting one is working in, for example if the meeting is the advisory sub-committee on consumer affairs that spent six hours discussing the labelling of packaging for toys, and even then did not arrive at any firm conclusions. When an interpreter knows they are working for people who genuinely need their services, who are intent on communicating, and when that communication becomes possible, the pleasure for the interpreter can be immense, particularly

– but not necessarily – if the participants acknowledge the interpreters' contribution to the proceedings. The fact that interpreters also have the opportunity of working with politicians, ambassadors, and other senior public figures, that sometimes they have the chance to witness historical events, is an added bonus, but is not the essence of the 'social' pleasure one can draw from the profession.

The intellectual pleasure itself is in turn twofold. First, the interpreter has the pleasure of dealing with the ideas expressed by the speakers. This pleasure is greater if the ideas themselves are intrinsically interesting. But even if they are not, even if the meeting is boring for an impartial observer (which the interpreter is, in a way), the interpreter can find an interest in dealing with different points of view and arguments, with the varying intellectual approaches and modes of expression of delegates.

Second, the pleasure is that of dealing with the linguistic problems created in interpreting. To be faced with a sentence in the source language with syntax incompatible with the target language; to be faced with an idiomatic saying that is untranslatable; to be faced with sentences of Kafkaesque or Proustian proportions and to have the task of providing it in digestible segments for your delegates; to be faced with all such tasks is rather like being faced with a chess problem. It is an abstract, intellectual problem to be solved, for its own sake and for the pleasure of it. Interpreting is like playing a game.

Moreover, the fact that interpreting is like playing a game provides, I think, the answer to another question put to men interpreters like myself. The question itself is a sexist one, harking back to times when men were supposed to have responsible, decision-making functions and women were supposed to have subordinate jobs with a secretarial, non-executive function. It is, 'Isn't it frustrating *for a man* to be in a job where you don't manage something, where you don't have an executive function?'. Setting aside the anachronistic nature of the question, one must reply to it by stressing that it is based, again, on a misapprehension about the pleasure to be obtained from interpreting. True, being an interpreter can imply a high degree of responsibility: a meeting or a negotiation can, in an extreme case, succeed or fail depending on the interpretation. Yet the interpreter's intellectual pleasure comes not from wielding power or exercising responsibility, but from the abstract, game-playing nature of their activity. And playing games is just as attractive to men as it is to women.

Not only can interpreting be compared to chess but it even has an advantage over chess. On a chessboard there is an objective situation with fixed rules applying. The only thing that will determine which player wins is their reasoning power. Interpreting, however, as we have mentioned, is not a pure science. True, there are many aspects of interpreting where you can apply an objective, analytical approach. But there are also aspects that are more subjective, where the interpreter must use their discretion in the translation they opt for, or where they must react in an audience specific or a situation specific way. In this sense, interpreting is rather closer to a more intuitive game such as bridge. During the auction in bridge, a player bids without knowing the cards of their partner, or of their opponents. Similarly, the simultaneous interpreter must interpret a speaker without having heard the totality of what the speaker intends to say. Then in both the auction and the play of the cards in bridge, there is room for psychological assessment, for trying out hypotheses, for playing a percentage game. The same goes for interpreting.

Interpreting is thus an activity that combines the social pleasure of helping people to communicate with the intellectual pleasure of dealing with ideas and language, an intellectual pleasure which may be based upon the intrinsic interest of the ideas discussed, or which may also be an abstract, game-playing pleasure, marrying both objective, analytical reasoning and more intuitive or creative thought processes.

Glossary

Active language: A language into which an interpreter is capable of interpreting (cf. 'passive language'). See p. 8.

Active listening: Constant attention to the meanings or ideas expressed by a speaker, beyond the forms used to express them; cf. *l'écoute du sens* ('listening to meaning') in Seleskovitch and Lederer (1989:16-22). See section on 'understanding', especially pp. 11-14.

Calque: A generic term for translations that reproduce source-language forms in the target language in situations where those forms are not normal in the target language; sometimes called 'loan translation' or, more generally, 'interference'. In the context of interpreting, reformulation techniques are designed to reduce calques.

Consecutive: Here used as a noun standing for 'consecutive interpreting', understood as the spoken rendering of a speech or speech fragment immediately after it has been pronounced.

Delegate: Here a generic term for anyone participating in a meeting, either speaking or listening, although in international settings it is assumed that most participants are representing their country. In the scope of this book, interpreters into language L are seen as working for the benefit of 'their' delegates, namely the L-speaking ones.

Internationalese: The jargon typical of international conferences and meetings, accepting multiple calques; here used in a pejorative sense, as something to be avoided by interpreters. See section on 'reformulation', especially p. 86.

Interpretation: The generic term for oral translation, here used to describe the *product* of the conference interpreter's activity.

Interpreting: The process by which an interpretation is produced, here understood as the *activity* of the conference interpreter.

Mother tongue: Here, an interpreter's best active language, independently of whether it is the language of either of their parents or even of their country of birth. In exceptional cases an interpreter may have two mother tongues. See pp. 8-9.

Multi-translation: Translation or interpreting involving work from a number of source languages, leading to different interferences from each source language. See section on 'reformulation', pp. 86.

Passive Language: A language out of which an interpreter is capable of interpreting (cf. 'active' and 'working' languages). See p. 8.

Pat phrases: Phrases that can be uttered as almost automatic responses to certain cues. In interpreting, the interpreter should have a repertoire of such phrases, in accordance with the nature of the setting and the field being discussed. See section on 'pat phrases', pp. 114-15.

Retour: An interpretation where the interpreter is working into an active language other than their mother tongue (*retour* is French for 'return' or 'going back'). See pp. 120-122.

Reformulation: The general practice of modifying the form of an utterance so as to reproduce its meaning in another language. See pp. 80-91.

Relay: The use of one interpretation as a source for others; used in situations where a meeting is multilingual and not all the interpreters understand all of the languages. The interpreter providing the source for other interpreters is called the 'relay', as is the interpretation itself. Relay can be used in consecutive and in simultaneous. See p. 9 (terms used) and the section on relay, pp. 122-124.

Rheme: The constituent of a sentence that adds most new information; i.e. whatever is said about the 'theme' (q.v.). See pp. 84-85.

Salami Technique: The technique of 'slicing up' a long or complicated sentence into shorter, more comprehensible sentences during the interpreting process. See pp. 91-95.

Simultaneous: Here used as a noun standing for 'simultaneous interpreting'.

Source Language: The language in which a speech is made in the original, and out of which the speech is to be interpreted. See p. 8.

Speaker: Here, the original speaker to be interpreted; not to be confused with the interpreter, even if the latter is 'speaking'.

Speech Types: Here, the simplest forms of the various speeches made at international conferences and meetings; not to be confused with the more general linguistic term *speech acts*, as found in the pragmatic analysis of discourse. See pp. 14-21.

Subject-Verb-Object: Here, the analysis of an utterance in terms of the basic structure X (subject) acts upon (verb) Y (object), allowing that the 'object' Y may in some cases be a complement (e.g. 'She is *poor*'). In interpreting, this mode of analysis need not be restricted to the level of clauses or sentences but should operate on the wider level of discourse. See pp. 23-24 (basic principles of consecutive) and pp. 44-46 (notetaking).

Target Language: The language into which a speech is to be put, and which the interpreter therefore speaks. See p. 8.

Theme: The first major constituent of a sentence; i.e. that which is talked about (cf. 'rheme'). See pp. 84-85.

Translation Unit: The unit of verbal and/or nonverbal signs that cannot be broken down into smaller elements in the translation process.

Unit of Meaning: Here used in the sense of Seleskovitch and Lederer's *unité de sens* (1989:246-247): a cognitive representation in the mind of the interpreter of the intended meaning of the speaker, formed from the words spoken by the speaker and the application to those words of contextual and background information available to the interpreter. See pp. 73-76.

Word-for-Word: An interpretation that follows the form of the source speech as closely as the target grammar will allow, without using reformulation.

Working Languages: The sum of an interpreter's active and passive languages. See p. 8.

Further Reading

Compiled by Miriam Shlesinger, Anthony Pym, David Sawyer and Zsuzsa G. Láng.

Although the aim of this book is to explain no more than the *practice* of conference interpreting, note should be made of the growing body of research in this field. The following list brings together classical prescriptive texts, some contributions from empirical research, and books elaborating the main theoretical approaches. By no means exhaustive, these notes are offered in the hope that instructors and students of interpreting may not only follow the research but also contribute to its future.

Books and Key Articles

Altman, Janet (ed.) (1987) *Teaching Interpreting: Study and Practice*, London: Centre for Information on Language Teaching and Research.

Barik, Henri C. (1973) 'Simultaneous Interpretation: Temporal and Quantitative Data', *Language and Speech* 16:237-270; and 'Simultaneous Interpretation: Qualitative and Linguistic Data', *Language and Speech* 18: 272-297. The main texts of Barik's classical research. While the study of interpreters' output has undergone considerable changes since these early studies, these papers were groundbreaking at the time.

Bowen, David and Margareta Bowen (1980) *Steps to Consecutive Interpretation*, Washington DC: Pen and Booth.

Bowen, David and Margareta Bowen (eds) (1990) *Interpreting – Yesterday, Today and Tomorrow*, Binghamton: SUNY.

Chernov, Ghelly (1987) *Osnovi sinhronogo perevoda* [The Foundations of Simultaneous Translation], Moscow: Vissia skola.

Collados Aís, Angela (1998) *La evaluación de la calidad en interpretación simultánea: La importancia de la comunicación no verbal*, Peligros, Granada: Comares.

Danks, Joseph H., Gregory M. Shreve, Stephen B. Fountain and Michael K. McBeath (eds) (1997) *Cognitive Processes in Translation and Interpreting*, Thousand Oaks / London / New Delhi: Sage Publications.

Déjean-Le Féal, Karla (1997) 'Simultaneous interpretation with "training wheels"', *Meta* 42(4): 616-621.

Delisle, Jean and Judith Woodsworth (1995) *Translators through History*, Amsterdam & Philadelphia: Benjamins. Chapter Nine deals with the history of interpreters, as well as countless fascinating anecdotes about the numerous roles played by translators.

Dollerup, Cay and Leo Ceelen (1996) *A Corpus of Consecutive Interpreting in Danish, Dutch, English, French, German and Italian*, Copenhagen: Centre for

Translation Studies and Lexicography. Transcripts of speeches and renditions, for use in empirical research and possibly in demonstrations for teaching purposes.

Fabbro, Franco, Bruno Gran and Laura Gran (1991) 'Hemispheric specialization for semantic and syntactic components of language in simultaneous interpreters', *Brain and Language* 41:1-42.

Fabbro, Franco, Laura Gran, Gianpaolo Basso and Antonio Bava (1990) 'Cerebral lateralization in simultaneous interpretation', *Brain and Language* 39:69-89.

Falbo, Caterina, Mariachiara Russo, and Francesco Straniero Sergio (eds) (1999) *Interpretazione simultanea e consecutiva: problemi teorici e metodologie didattiche*, Milan: Hoepli. Based on a series of lectures given in the Trieste school in 1995, these introductions form a comprehensive manual for students, covering historical, neurological and sociolinguistic aspects of both consecutive and simultaneous.

Gambier, Yves, Daniel Gile and Christopher Taylor (eds) (1997) *Conference Interpreting: Current Trends in Research*, Amsterdam and Philadelphia: John Benjamins. Proceedings of a 1994 conference organized to assess the state of the art in conference interpreting research, presented as the coordinated results of round tables dealing with methodology, culture, neurolinguistic and cognitive aspects, quality assessment and training.

Gerver, David and H. Wallace Sinaiko (eds) (1978) *Language Interpretation and Communication*, New York: Plenum. A classical collection of essays from a conference aimed at creating an interface between psychologists and interpreting researchers.

Gile, Daniel (1995a) *Basic Concepts and Models for Interpreter and Translator Training*, Amsterdam & Philadelphia: Benjamins. This volume gives special attention to conference interpreting, particularly in chapters dealing with 'effort models', 'coping tactics' and the 'gravitational model' of language competence. The theoretical issues are very clearly explained and are followed by useful suggestions on pertinent class activities.

Gile, Daniel (1995b) *Regards sur la recherche en interprétation de conférence*, Lille: Presses Universitaires de Lille. An analysis of conference interpreting research issues, including research topics and the research community.

Gile, Daniel (ed.) (1995) *Interpreting Research* (= *Target* 7.1), Amsterdam & Philadelphia: Benjamins. Articles on the state of interpreting research, with reflections on interdisciplinarity and possible future directions.

Gran, Laura and Christopher Taylor (eds) (1990). *Aspects of Applied and Experimental Research on Conference Interpretation*, Udine: Campanotto.

Gran, Laura and John Dodds (eds) (1989). *The Theoretical and Practical Aspects of Teaching Conference Interpretation*, Udine: Campanotto.

Herbert, Jean (1952) *Manuel de l'interprète: comment on devient interprète de conférences*, Geneva: Librairie de l'Université. A dated but still authoritative guide.

Hyöna, J., J. Tommola and A. M. Alaja (1995) 'Pupil dilation as a measure of processing load in simultaneous interpreting and other language tasks', *The Quarterly*

Journal of Experimental Psychology 48 A: 598-612. Obscure research for the curious.

Iliescu Gheorghiu, Catalina (2001) *Introducción a la interpretación. La modalidad consecutiva,* Alicante: Publicaciones de la Universidad de Alicante. A useful pedagogical introduction to consecutive.

Lambert, Sylvie (1990) 'Simultaneous interpreters: one ear may be better than two', *The Interpreters' Newsletter* 2: 11-16.

Karttunen, Frances (1994) *Between Worlds: Interpreters, Guides and Survivors,* New Brunswick NJ: Rutgers University Press.

Kohn, Kurt and Sylvia Kalina (1996) 'The Strategic Dimension of Interpreting', *Meta* 41(1):118-38.

Kurz, Ingrid (1996) *Simultandolmetschen als Gegenstand der interdisziplären Forschung,* Vienna: WUV-Universitätsverlag. One of the broadest and best-researched overviews of Interpretation Studies, covering the history of simultaneous, quality, cognitive science, empirical studies, personality factors and neurophysiological research.

Kurz, Ingrid and Angela Moisl (eds) (1997) *Berufsbilder für Übersetzer und Dolmetscher: Perspektiven nach dem Studium,* Vienna: WUV-Universitätsverlag. A collection of essays on written mostly from the personal perspective, covering nearly all aspects of the profession as well as related careers such as journalism.

Kurz, Ingrid (2001) 'Conference Interpreting: Quality in the Ears of the User', *Meta* 46(2):394-409.

Lambert, Sylvie and Barbara Moser-Mercer (eds) (1994) *Bridging the Gap: Empirical Research in Simultaneous Interpretation,* Amsterdam & Philadelphia: Benjamins. Papers on empirical research, mostly adopting the methods of cognitive psychology and addressing various educational contexts. The volume also includes data on bilingual cerebralization and interesting tidbits like measures of interpreters' blood-pressure and heart-rate patterns while working.

Láng, Zsuzsa G. (2002) *Tolmácsolás felsofokon. A hivatásos tolmácsok képzésérol* (A handbook for the training of professional interpreters). Budapest: Scholastica.

Lederer, Marianne (1981) *La traduction simultanée. Expérience et théorie,* Paris: Minard.

Lederer, Marianne (1994) *La traduction aujourd'hui. Le modèle interprétatif,* Vances: Hachette F.L.E. A summary of the ESIT approach to interpreting (deverbalization, meaning transfer, re-expression), presented as a general theory applicable to all kinds of translation.

Lee, Tae-Hyung (1999) 'Speech Proportion and Accuracy in Simultaneous Interpretation from English into Korean', *Meta* 44(4):560-72.

Matyssek, Heinz (1989) *Handbuch der Notizentechnik für Dolmetscher,* Heidelberg: Julius Groos. A maximalist approach, developing comprehensive symbolization systems.

Moser, Peter (1996) 'Expectations of Users of Conference Interpretation', *Interpreting* 1(2):145-78.

Moser-Mercer, Barbara, Uli Frauenfelder, Beatriz Casado and Alexander. Künzli

(2000) 'Searching to Define Expertise in Interpreting', in Birgitta Englund Dimi-trova and Kenneth Hyltenstam (eds) *Language Processing and Simultaneous Interpretation: Interdisciplinary Perspectives*, Amsterdam and Philadelphia: John Benjamins, pp. 107-31.

Paradis, Michel (1994) 'Toward a Neurolinguistic Theory of Simultaneous Transla-tion: The Framework', *International Journal of Psycholinguistics* 9(3):161-90.

Pearl, Steven (1995) 'Lacuna, Myth and Shibboleth in the Teaching of Simultane-ous Interpreting', *Perspectives: Studies in Translatology* 3(1):161-90.

Pöchhacker, Franz (1993) 'From Knowledge to Text: Coherence in Simultaneous Interpreting', Yves Gambier and Jorma Tommola (eds) *Translation and Knowl-edge: SSOTT IV,* Turku: University of Turku, Centre for Translation and Interpreting, 87-100.

Pöchhacker, Franz (1994) *Simultandolmetschen als komplexes Handeln*, Tübingen: Narr. A functionalist critique and analysis of ideas and concepts of simultaneous interpreting, placed in the context of the model conference as the pertinent envi-ronment, followed up by a description and analysis of a sample conference.

Pöchhacker, Franz (2001) 'Quality Assessment in Conference and Community In-terpreting', *Meta* 46(2):410-25.

Pöchhacker, Franz, and Miriam Shlesinger (2001) *The Interpreting Studies Reader*, London and New York: Routledge. A benchmark collection of seminal articles covering numerous aspects of the field, organized into thematic sections and giving extensive bibliographical references.

Roland, Ruth A. (1999) *Interpreters as Diplomats. A Diplomatic History of the Role of Interpreters in World Politics*, Ottawa: University of Ottawa Press. Reprint of a 1982 book called *Translating World Affairs*, which focuses on much more than the role of interpreters as such.

Rozan, Jean-François (1956) *La prise de notes en interprétation consécutive,* Ge-neva: Georg. The classical 'minimalist' approach to note-taking in consecutive.

Salevsky, Heidemarie (1986) *Probleme des Simultandolmetschens: Eine Studie zur Handlungsspezifik*, Berlin: Akademie der Wissenschaften der DDR Zentral-institut für Sprachwissenschaft.

Salevsky, Heidemarie (1993) 'The Distinctive Nature of Interpreting Studies', *Tar-get: International Journal of Translation Studies* 5(2):149-67.

Seleskovitch, Danica and Marianne Lederer (1984) *Interpréter pour traduire*, Paris: Didier. Classical collection of articles on the main concepts of the approach de-veloped at the ESIT in Paris, many of which are at the base of the ideas elaborated in the present book: re-expression, reformulation, active listening (*l'écoute du sens*), units of meaning, etc.

Seleskovitch, Danica and Marianne Lederer (1989) *Pédagogie raisonnée de l'inter-prétation*, Brussels-Luxembourg: Opoce, Didier. Trans. Jacolyn Harmer (1995) *A Systematic Approach to Teaching Interpretation*, Silver Spring MD: Registry of Interpreters for the Deaf. Presentation and pedagogical explanation of the ESIT approach to conference interpreting, both consecutive and simultaneous. Pre-pared for the European Commission, the volume includes supplementary chapters on remote conferencing, student evaluation, and relations with linguistics.

Setton, Robin (1999) *Simultaneous Interpretation. A cognitive-pragmatic analysis.* Amsterdam & Philadelphia: Benjamins.

Shlesinger, Miriam (1989) 'Extending the Theory of Translation to Interpretation: Norms as a Case in Point', *Target: International Journal of Translation Studies* 1(1):111-16.

Shlesinger, Miriam (2000) 'Interpreting as a Cognitive Process: How Can We Know What Actually Happens?' Sonja Tirkkonen-Condit and Riitta Jääskeläinen (eds) *Tapping and Mapping the Processes of Translation and Interpreting. Outlooks on Empirical Research*, Amsterdam and Philadelphia: Benjamins, 3-15.

Snelling, David (1992) *Strategies for Simultaneous Interpreting from Romance Languages into English*, Udine: Campanotto. A survey of strategies for students working into their non-native language, insisting that one first interprets words, not meanings.

Szabari, Krisztina (1999) *Tolmácsolás. Bevezetés a tolmácsolás elméletébe és gyakorlatába* (Introduction to the Theory and Practice of Interpreting). Budapest: Scholastica.

Tommola, Jorma (ed.) *Topics in Interpreting Research*, Turku: University of Turku, Centre for Translation and Interpreting (available through St Jerome Publishing). Includes papers on cognitive aspects of the interpreting process, memory performance, and research methodology.

Van Besien, Fred (1999) 'Anticipation in Simultaneous Interpretation', *Meta* 44(2):250-259.

Zmudzki, Jerzy (1995) *Konsekutivdolmetschen: Handlungen-Operationen-Strategien*, Lublin: Wydawnictwo Uniwersytetu Marii-Sklodowskiek.

Journals

Interpreting. International Journal of Research and Practice in Interpreting (John Benjamins). Edited by Barbara Moser-Mercer and Dominic W. Massaro.

The IRN Bulletin. International Interpretation Research Information Network An independent informal network for the dissemination of information on conference interpretation research and theory. Edited by Daniel Gile and distributed electronically twice a year. Contact: e-mail: DGile@compuserve.com.

The Interpreters' Newsletter (Trieste).

The Translator (St. Jerome Publishing). Published twice a year; each issue usually has one article on an aspect of interpreting.

Further information can be found at the website of the AIIC: www.aiic.net.

Numerous articles have also been published in collective volumes on general translation research, as well as in journals specializing in neighbouring disciplines. The above list should thus be seen as a springboard, not as the deep end of interpreting research.

Index

abbreviations, in note-taking 41, 49-53
active language, defined 8
active listening 12-14
anticipation, in simultaneous 105f.
arrows, in note-taking 55-57
audience 98-100, and mother tongue 123

bilingual and multilingual meetings 7
booths 66, teamwork in 119-120

cerebral specialization, in simultaneous 67
chuchotage (whispered interpreting), defined 5, 68
completion of sentences 71
conference interpreting, defined 5
consecutive interpreting, defined 5; basic principles 11-38
context, in simultaneous 87-88
'cost-effective' (example) 82
cultural differences 3-4
Czech syntax (example) 84-85

efficiency, in simultaneous 95-98
equipment, in simultaneous 67ff.
ethics, in simultaneous 89, 102-103
examples, can be edited 25
explanation, in simultaneous 104-105
eye-contact, in consecutive 35, in simultaneous 66

Fabbro, Franco, & Laura Gran 67
false epithets 24
fast speakers 102-104

generalization, in simultaneous 101-102
German syntax, as false problem 106-107
glossaries 89, and technical meetings 8
'Golden rules' of simultaneous 72

headphones 67
'hops' (example) 87-88

international organizations 6
interpreters' interventions 19, no substantive addition 21, questions to speakers
34-35, 44, and speaker's mistakes 109-110
interpreting, defined 3, conference interpreting defined 4-5
intonation 36, in simultaneous 115-117

jokes, in simultaneous 111-112

Lambert, Sylvie 67
language choice, in note-taking 60-61
language switch, in simultaneous 124
layout, in note-taking 44-47
Lederer, Marianne 73-75
links, in speeches 28-29, in note-taking 41, 46, 53
lists, in note-taking 39, 43, verticality 48
logical connections 15-17, analysis of links 28-29

Matyssek, Heinz 49
memory, mnemonic techniques 29-33; key points 33, in note-taking 39-40
metaphors 112-114
missing information, in note-taking 49
mistakes, interpreter's 107-108, speaker's 108-110
modal verbs, in note-taking 42, 54-55
mother tongue 8-9

notepads 40
note-taking 39-65, notepads 40, layout 44-47, language choice 60-61, timing
61-63, reading back 64
numbers, in note-taking 42-43, 58, in simultaneous 117f.

omission, in simultaneous 102

passive language, defined 8
passive listening 13
'pat phrases' 114
pauses, in simultaneous 115-116
point of view 23, in note-taking 41-42
pressure on interpreters 116
proper names, in note-taking 43, 51

questions to speakers 34-35, 44
quotations 112

reading written texts 103
recapitulation, in simultaneous 104
re-expression 33-37
reformulation 80-91, stylistic 82-83, and target language 83, salami technique 91-95, efficiency 95-98
relay, defined 9, 112-124
repetition, avoided 35, in simultaneous 97
retour, defined 9, 120-122
Rozan, Jean-François 45, 49

salami technique 91-95
Seleskovitch, Danica 73-75
sentences, in simultaneous 70-71, 81ff., salami technique 91-95
simplification, in simultaneous 98-101
simultaneous interpreting, defined 5, 66-127, 'Golden Rules' 72, reformulation 80-91, salami technique 91-95
source language, defined 8
speech structure, in note-taking 40
speech type 14-21; pro-and-con 15-1616; one-sided 16-17; narrative 17-18; descriptive 18; polemical 18-19; rhetorical 19-21, in note-taking 40
split attention, in simultaneous 68-70
stress (emphasis), in note-taking 55, in simultaneous 115-117
subject-verb-object (SVO) analysis 23-24, in note-taking 41, 44-45
summarizing, in simultaneous 104
symbols, in note-taking 49-50, 52, 57-59
syntax, as giving meaning 84, Czech 84-85, simplified in simultaneous 93, German 106-107

target language, defined 8; developing skills 37
technical meetings 8
TGV (example) 105
time constraints 5-6, in note-taking 39, 61-63, in simultaneous: starting 72, 76-78, distance from speaker 80f., efficiency in simultaneous 96f., fast speakers 103, in relay 123

understanding 11-14, words not understood 11-12, 87-89; understanding meaning 12-14
unit of meaning 73-76
unknown words 87-89

verbs, tense in note-taking 53-54, modals in note-taking 54-55
voice and volume level, in simultaneous 68

whispered interpreting (*chuchotage*), defined 5, 68
word-for-word translation 85-86
words not understood 11-12
work modes, organizational vs. private 7
working language, defined 8
written texts 103